MW01672690

Embracing the Heart, Engaging the Mind:

Universal Stories of Resilience

(65 Stories with Commentary)

Joseph R. Dunn, Ph.D.

Disclaimer: This work (ISBN 978-0-578-01156-1) and Psychology Etcetera Press and Publishing do not offer psychological, medical or any other professional advice, diagnosis, or treatment in any manner whatsoever.

Published and printed in the United States of America by Psychology Etcetera Press (PsychEtc.com).

If you are unable to order this book from your local bookseller, you may order directly from the publisher or author. For permissions, bulk purchases or other information visit www.psychetc.com or refer to order information at the end of the book, page 207.

Catalogue-in-Publication Data
Dunn, Joseph Richard
Embracing the heart, engaging the mind: universal stories of resilience, 65 Stories with commentary

1.Psychological Resilience 2. Folklore/Literature 3. Spirituality/Religion 4. Teaching and Wisdom Stories 5. Positive Psychology 6. Psychotherapy 7. Psychology 8. Counseling 9. Communications 10. Business and Human Resources

ISBN 978-0-578-01156-1

Dedication

Dedicated with love to my mother, Rosebud McRae Dunn, and in memory of my father, Joe L. Dunn. I am grateful to my mother for her encouragement, support, and love of family. As a mother, grandmother, great-grandmother, wife, aunt...she has always embraced our family and bonded it together. As a retired elementary school librarian, she loves children's literature. Metaphorically, she has always been very committed to make sure that books stayed bound, bonded, as well. Many of her former students warmly remember Miss Rosebud for the stories that she read them during their library periods.

I thank my father for introducing me to the world of stories, the power of the spoken word, and the meaning of oral tradition. Many in his community recognized him as a good storyteller and one who reserved the right to embellish at will. He communicated much family history through stories. However, few realize that he created a series of "Bear Tales" with a cast of characters that he only shared at bedtime with my son, my sister, and me when we were each young. Through his Bear Tales, he communicated important life lessons and values.

Acknowledgements

First and foremost, I owe a special debt of appreciation to Elizabeth Derrick Clayton, friend and colleague, for her support, encouragement and occasional prodding to complete this work. Her authentic interest in my writing and assistance in listening, editing, and proofreading are deeply appreciated.

In addition, I am grateful to my classmate, dating back to graduate school, David Norris, for generously sharing his time and suggestions. I thank my sister, Dr. Joy R. Dunn, for her recommendations. Further, I am most appreciative to Janice Detrick for her editorial assistance.

I am very grateful to Dr. William F. Fry, Jr. for his continuing support and encouragement of my writing over many years. Though his humility prevents his accepting much praise, I am indebted to him much more than he realizes.

Also, I thank my son, Jonathan, and daughter-in-law, Teresa, not only for the love and joy that they give me but for producing a wonderful audience of three additional readers, my grandchildren, Katie, Bailey Rose, and Isaac.

I must acknowledge my friend and colleague, Dr. Waleed A. Salameh, who shares a love of teaching stories and humor. His ancestral leanings are rooted in the Middle East where stories have been orally communicated from generation to generation for millennia. He introduced me to Joha who is a character presented in several of the stories.

Furthermore, I thank my extended family for sharing stories of life. While growing up, I looked forward to family gatherings. They were special days filled with storytelling by uncles, aunts, cousins ....

Contents

"The story is as old as our life on this planet.
It anchors each of us to our family and
to the place where we live.
In *Embracing the Heart, Engaging the Mind*
Joseph Dunn gathers interesting stories
from throughout the world
and suggests how we can relate them
to our own life."

William Ferris, PhD, Professor,
University of North Carolina, Chapel Hill,
Former Chairman of the
National Endowment for the Humanities

Preface

The preface can offer insight into a book or be tedious. In this case it is both. The author would prefer to begin with the Introduction; however, he shall defer to protocol. Besides, the section does provide information that can be fundamental and crucial to a reader's understanding of the book.

This book contains a diverse array of versions of sixty-five stories from around the world. Most of the tales date back several centuries and generation after generation has passed them down to us. Some of the stories have biographical and historical roots. A few are ancient and some are modern. Numerous stories come from multiple sources with variations recorded in diverse cultures and nations. Many of the tales originated in the Middle East, but they have spread throughout the world and claimed by various cultures. The collection includes Sufi, Zen, Buddhist, Hebrew, Jewish (Rabbinical), and Christian stories as well as Eastern, Middle Eastern, European, African, Native American, and American stories.

They come from a lifetime collection, an accumulation that began long before the collector was consciously aware of the compilation. Many of the stories represent revised and adapted versions. Each chapter presents a set of stories that deal with a principle that promotes psychological resilience.

Please note that the author shares a sentiment expressed by Joan Baez. On one of her albums, *Blessed are...*, she offered a comment about the lyrics to the songs. She said that any changes were either "intentional or otherwise." The same applies to previous versions of the stories in this collection.

Terms:

Although psychology as a discipline in the United States has focused primarily upon pathology for the past six decades, recently an expanding interest in qualities that help one cope and adapt effectively has emerged into a movement within the discipline. "Psychological resilience" is one of many terms that overlap in meaning and have much in common. "Positive Psychology" is another term and the most popular. I prefer the term "psychological resilience" and as used in this work the term incorporates psychological survival and thriving.

No matter what term is used, the movement focuses on building upon psychological strengthens as opposed to expelling debilities. It emphasizes potential, growth, and well being rather than psychopathology. The movement asserts that the absence of mental illness does not mean that one enjoys optimum mental health or well-being. Also, developing resilience has been compared to building the "psychological immune system." [For a more detailed discussion of the previous two paragraphs, please refer to the addendums.]

Boundaries and Audience:

Embracing the Heart, Engaging the Mind presents stories, which serve as a base to discuss and illustrate psychological resilience. The discussion is presented in the form of commentary, which expands the stories and offers observations. Often the commentary refers to psychological studies and literature. The comments cite lessons and applications offered by the stories. The book does not attempt to present a comprehensive review of the literature on resilience, nor does it attempt to identify all of the qualities of psychological resilience but rather some of the most important.

The author's background in psychology, theology, and life experience tends to influence the comments as well as his observations and experience in psychotherapy, marriage counseling, psychological assessment, and teaching. Further, his interests, which include biographies, documentaries, mind/body health, spirituality, and humor, shape the commentaries. Those with other backgrounds and interests could present alternative comments. Readers are invited to apply additional commentary that may be applicable from personal experience or knowledge.

Though scholarship and scientific research are definitely appreciated and respected, *Embracing the Heart, Engaging the Mind* is not intended to speak to academics nor behavioral scientists, though they are most welcomed as readers. Nor is the book addressed to those who seek immediate, overly simplistic, "pop," solutions to serious life concerns.

The book is intended for a general, multidisciplinary audience and for readers who prefer more substantive content than "pop" writing offers without the arduous jargon of academic literature. The work is meant for serious readers of varied ages who value diverse stories and practical comments communicated in a casual and more informal than scholarly form. Students of psychology and all other disciplines that value stories are welcomed as readers.

Introduction

In the beginning, before there were psychologists, consultants, and experts, there were stories. Throughout the ages, wise teachers, clerics, and statesmen have embraced stories, parables, myths, proverbs, and folktales to comfort, coach, and celebrate as well as to encourage, entertain, and edify.

Stories teach great lessons of wisdom even as they sometimes expose our folly. They alter preconceived attitudes and open new vistas. Stories can help us see when we may not listen and listen when we may not see. Stories offer new instruction as well as remind us and reinforce lessons that we have previously learned. Stories teach lessons of psychological, social, and spiritual significance.

Stories often provoke questions or thought that open doors— doors that may lead to solutions. This resource aims to present a variety of ideas clothed in an array of stories that the recipient may apply to his or her life as may be appropriate, and as one may choose.

Stories invite us to examine our personal lives as well as life collectively. They remind us of realities and possibilities of what can be. Stories may unearth or reveal what we know but do not yet know that we know.

Stories as Gifts

I can imagine an ancient, remote tribe setting, where elders communicated their cultural heritage while sitting around the campfire. The elders began the ritual of telling stories by chanting, “Our stories are true and our stories are untrue. But none are false, and all are spoken in the language of venerable wisdom. Know that our stories are precious gifts bequeathed to guide you and your progeny.”

Look to the Sea

The spark that ignited the inspiration for this work occurred while watching an educational television documentary many years ago. The story is not presented for its historical accuracy. The historicity is debatable. The story is presented because it speaks metaphorical truth and addresses the nature of the human condition. The story may not be real, but it presents truth.

The documentary was about the Irish potato famine in the 1840’s. The narrator and those interviewed spoke of how potatoes were essential as a food source and vital for survival. They went into detail about how there had been an overabundance of potatoes in previous years but that after a fog lifted in the spring of 1845 there appeared the first signs of “the blight.” The potatoes rotted and continued to decay. It was noted that in Ireland they relied primarily upon a single variety of potato, the lumper, which was highly productive.

The famine continued for several years and conditions deteriorated until the people were literally dying of starvation. At first, they survived, but as the famine continued people became weaker and malnourished and were susceptible to disease. Of course, some migrated during that time and some charitable groups sent grain, but it was not enough. The point came when people would eat anything to stay alive. As the catastrophe progressed, people foraged for roots, leaves, and grass until they were depleted. Rodents brought a premium. The seed potatoes sent to them to plant new crops were consumed as food.

Near the conclusion of the documentary, one of the interviewees stated that the starvation and suffering could have been prevented. According to him, an abundant supply of fish swam in the waters offshore, but that the Irish had always been farmers and fixated their expectations upon looking to the land to sustain them.

Initially, the story reminds us of how quickly life conditions can change. Conditions can change from fortune to misfortune or misfortune to fortune precipitously. For years, there had been an overabundance of potatoes. How quickly their lives changed. Universally, individuals and cultures experience this story; however, that is not the reason that the story struck me.

Immediately, I found the story disquieting and unsettling! It was poignant and penetrating. It touched my being. How distressing for people to experience such an appalling tragedy and depravity, unnecessarily. I found the documentary's conclusion, if it were true or even partially true, unacceptable. I wanted to hear that some enterprising person had said, "It is time to quit farming and start fishing."

The story spoke to me in a manner similar to a parable or other literature. It speaks metaphorical truth about the human condition. The skeleton or motif of this story expands millennia. This story is not just about what may have happened in Ireland in the 1840's. It not only speaks to those of us of Irish heritage, it speaks to all people, everywhere, for all time.

The story was haunting because it invited me to examine my life. Stories invite us to examine our lives. Although my struggles are not comparable in severity to what the Irish faced at that time, I wondered, "Am I looking to the land when I should be looking to the sea?"

To borrow two applicable song titles: Am I looking "Right in the Wrong Direction" or "Looking for Love in all the Wrong Places." Am I experiencing a deficit or loss when there is a solution in sight? Am I experiencing deprivation in some area of my life— whether physical, psychological, social, material, or spiritual— when a bountiful resource is available, just offshore?

At times looking to the land will lead to appropriate solutions. However, the purpose of this work is to encourage us to open our hearts and minds to turn and look to the sea as well. The famine story points out the need for psychological resilience. Psychological resilience does not refer to the absence of struggles, hardships, or challenges but rather using strengths and talents to overcome adversity. The following stories are more uplifting and presented to encourage and promote psychological resilience and thriving. The flexibility to identify choices, confront challenges, and seize opportunities involves embracing and engaging the heart and mind to unite in harmony.

Heart and Mind:

I shall refrain from discussing or arguing detailed differences between the mind and brain, or mind and heart. I believe that most have enough understanding to comprehend the contents of this book without extended elaboration.

I shall note that recent research has pointed to the importance of coherence between the functioning of the heart and brain. Though separate organs, the heart and brain interact to a great extent by way of various neurological and bio-chemical connections. In an interview with the author, the late Dr. Paul Pearsall said, "The brain is critical to our survival, but our heart is essential to our thriving. The heart has been essentially left out of the often lethal alliance between the brain and its body."

Today, scientists speak of the intelligence of the heart and emotional aspects of the brain. When the heart and mind are in sync or in-phase there is less stress, greater clarity of thought, and stability of emotions. Awareness expands, reaction times increase, and listening improves. When the coherence breaks down and the intellect and emotions are out-of-phase, there is greater stress. Thinking, perceptions, and decision-making processes deteriorate.

The effect of uniting the heart and mind has the impact that Gestalt psychology addresses: the whole is greater than the sum of the parts. It is my belief that teaching stories offer one avenue to promote coherence between the mind and heart. I like Nelson Mandela's observation, "A good head and a good heart are always a formidable combination."

Summary of Chapters

Chapter I: The first chapter is about diamonds and gold. It is also about other treasures such as courage, hope, and compassion. It offers stories with commentary on discovering and discerning what is of value.

Chapter II: Like parents, authors prefer not to acknowledge favorites; however, the second chapter is one of my favorites. It deals with examples of establishing, building, and transforming relationships. Much of our fulfillment in life is contingent upon our relationships with others. The chapter offers some innovatively practical insights spiced with a touch of romance.

Chapters III and IV: Chapters III and IV can be viewed from the perspective of the famous Serenity Prayer. Another viewpoint is the attitude expressed by Viktor Frankl when he discussed free will and determinism and observed that we are not free from conditions but we do have a choice regarding how we confront conditions.

The stories in Chapter III involve accepting reality in both the mind and heart. Chapter IV deals with the will or courage to change what we can.

Chapter V: Everyone faces "slings and arrows" or obstacles and detours in life. Chapter V presents stories dealing with decisions about life conflicts, struggles, and dilemmas. Furthermore, it addresses The Serenity Prayer regarding "the wisdom to know the difference" and may be viewed as the third chapter in the series.

Chapter VI: There is much folly in life, so we may as well recognize it in ourselves and others and make the best of it. In some families, Folly and Wisdom are twins. Chapter VI deals with folly but also contains much wisdom. It includes stories of the rabbi and citizens of Chelm, Joha or Nasrudin stories as well as Sufi stories.

Chapter VII: If the law of supply and demand applies to attitudes and emotions as well as economics, then civility should be selling at a premium on the commodity exchange. Dealing with anger is inevitable in life. Everyone experiences anger; however, we do have choices as to how we accept it and whether we allow it to consume us.

Chapter VIII: Chapter VIII presents stories that a sage or judicious mentor might offer. It presents stories of wisdom and the discovery of resourceful solutions.

Chapter IX: Chapter IX presents one persons viewpoint upon humankinds tenacity to not only survive but prevail. Also included are additional concluding comments.

Final Words: Chapter IX is followed by closing comments which connect the end of the work with the beginning. Final Words is the formal end of the book.

Addendums: The addendums are more psychologically oriented and go into more detail on psychological aspects of resilience. Addendum I presents more terminology associated with psychological resilience and why the term is preferred. Addendum II offers more stories, as well as historical and research information on psychological resilience for those who may be interested. Addendum III offers specific, practical recommendations that promote resilience and thriving. Addendum IV cites additional resources and references.

The addendums are followed by information about the author and order/contact information.

I: Assessing Treasure

1. **The Messiah**
2. **The Bridge**
3. **The Rosetta Stone**
4. **Shakespeare's New Place**
5. **The Perfect Mate**
6. **Happiness**
7. **Two-Hundred Pounds**

The first group of stories deals with recognizing and appreciating treasure— that which possesses value. Not everything in life is of equal value; it is important to sort out and prioritize what is of worth.

One may have to embark upon a journey to discover or access treasure. One may have access to great treasure but not realize it or appreciate it. One may have access to vast treasure but its potential is in emergent form as a seedling that needs water, sunshine, and fertile soil to mature into a full-grown plant. What is valuable at one time or place may seem worthless at another.

As we look outward, we may direct our search toward knowing and appreciating treasure that is available; we may recognize fortune that may be accessible. As we look inward, we may identify and value that which we possess that is precious and thus realize what we have to offer and share with others.

Story 1: The Messiah

A rabbi was traveling in a foreign land. As evening drew near, he spotted a monastery ahead. He approached the gate and asked if he might spend the night. The abbot was pleased to offer the stranger food and lodging.

The next morning the abbot called the rabbi aside and requested that he might ask the rabbi a question. The rabbi complied. The abbot told of how the number of monks in the monastery had declined over the years and he feared that eventually the monastery would have to close. He said, "I've tried everything I know to recruit and retain monks but nothing has been successful. The monks are becoming discouraged and beginning to bicker, find fault, blame one another, and criticize me." The abbot inquired, "What advice can you offer?" The rabbi said, "I've only been among you for a short while, but I can offer one suggestion. Call a meeting of the monks and tell them that the Messiah is among you!" The abbot said, "How exciting. I had no idea. Tell me, who is the Messiah?" The rabbi said I cannot tell you, but if you do as I say, your monastery will flourish."

That evening the abbot called the group of monks together and made the announcement, "The Messiah is among us." Immediately after the announcement, the monks began to chatter with excitement: "Who is the Messiah? Who could it be? Could it be Brother Robert? Surely not, but he has some devout qualities. Could it be Brother James? He shows great compassion for the poor. Could it be Brother Peter? Could it be the abbot? Could, could it be me?"

As the monks went about their duties, they began to look at one another differently. They saw qualities in one another that they had not seen before. They felt honored that the Messiah was among their group. Morale transformed. The monastery began to grow again as more new members were attracted.

Comments:

As with most of our stories, this one presents a serious challenge. The abbot is facing the decline and possible demise of the monastery to which he had likely devoted his life. The rabbi was like a consultant, an authority from out of town. He offered a fresh perspective that altered how the monks viewed one another. Instead of finding fault and criticizing, they began to search for affirming qualities. When we recognize possibilities in others and ourselves, then our attitudes, feelings, and interpersonal relationships change.

I enjoy reading biographies and watching biographical documentaries. The number of people who have achieved greatness that had a parent or mentor who repeatedly told them that they were special or would achieve greatness stands out.

One example is Picasso. Picasso's mother repeatedly told him that whatever he did he would be great. She said, "If you become a soldier you'll be a general. If you become a priest you'll be Pope."

Howard Hughes who made history for advances in aviation had parents who applauded his mechanical inquiry. They were pleased when he would take machines apart to see how they worked and put them back together. When young Howard attached a motor to his bicycle, which was reported to be the first motorized bicycle, his mother called the local paper which printed the story and encouraged her son's ingenuity.

The person does not have to be a parent or grandparent. A spouse, colleague, teacher or mentor may serve the purpose. But a selfless, loving person who has another's interest at heart and sees possibilities in another, recognizing the germinating seed of some special quality and nourishes and cultivates it toward its ultimate expression of maturation is a powerful influence. Such a person's contribution may not be widely publicized. It may not be commonly recognized but nevertheless is of great value.

Essentially, what the rabbi did was offer the abbot and monks hope by having them focus upon their strengths and abilities. Nothing changed except their perception. However, changing their perception transformed their perspectives of themselves and others. Sharing an alternative perspective with those who are receptive may be a gift to be treasured. Benjamin Disraeli said, "The greatest good you can do for another is not just to share your riches but to reveal to him his own."

Story 2: The Bridge

Most of the stories in this collection are adapted, revised, and told in various forms in numerous cultures. The following story has versions from England, The Netherlands, Austria and other countries. There is one version in *Tales from the 1001 Nights* entitled "The Ruined Man Who Became Rich Again."

A cobbler who lived in a small village in the North Country had a recurring dream. He dreamed that he should go to the great bridge in the capitol city, which would result in leading him to a vast treasure. The dream recurred night after night and he told his wife that he felt compelled to go to the capitol and visit the bridge. After hearing him repeat his dream for weeks, his wife urged him to go to the bridge. He traveled a long distance and finally arrived at the bridge early one morning. He did not know what he was supposed to do, so he walked back and forth across the bridge for a while, then stood, and then sat for a while. He repeated the cycle over and over. He waited and waited until his fatigue overcame his excitement.

Finally, about dusk, a guard came up to the cobbler and said that he had watched the cobbler all day and that the stranger's behavior appeared most suspicious. The guard asked the cobbler to state his business. The cobbler was embarrassed and said that the guard would not believe him. The guard demanded to know the reason for the cobbler's peculiar behavior. The cobbler divulged his recurring dream and his urge to come to the bridge.

The guard laughed and said, "How ridiculous. You are a silly man. You cannot believe your dreams. I had a dream last night, too. It directed me to go to a cobbler's house in the North Country. The vision showed a great chest of treasure buried in the middle of the cobbler's basement. But I am not silly enough to go off on such a foolish adventure." The cobbler rushed home. He burst through the front door, explaining to his wife what had happened as they descended the steps to the basement. As you might suppose, as they dug there in the basement together, they uncovered a treasure chest of enormous value.

Comments:

There are several interesting elements to this story. The cobbler wrestled with whether or not to trust his dream. Should one place trust in a dream? Is it wise or foolish? Note that the cobbler did not act prematurely or on first impulse, but waited. In addition, there is the timely support offered by the wife that encouraged him to follow his dream. Dreams are fragile. Unknowingly, friends or loved ones may discourage another from pursuing a dream. Another point is that, in the process of following his dream, the cobbler stood on the bridge waiting and did not know what to expect. Doubts arose. Should he have trusted his dream? His intuition told him to follow his dream. He had no business plan or procedure manual to guide him.

Furthermore, the bridge symbolizes connection. Perhaps it represents connecting possibility with reality— what "can be" with "what is." The cobbler encountered ridicule from the guard. It did not make sense to the guard who was a strict realist. Without even realizing it, the guard played a major role in helping the cobbler fulfill his dream— something in which the guard did not believe.

What do you suppose would have happened if the cobbler had consulted his customers, friends, and acquaintances about whether he should follow his dream? Most likely they would have discouraged him. They would probably have offered the same advice as the guard at the bridge. He was most fortunate to have a wife with whom to share his dream and one who understood the importance of dreams. Some spouses would have considered the dream impractical and a threat to their security.

Note that the cobbler had to travel away from home, alone, in order to discover the treasure that he already possessed, the treasure that he had possessed for years and years. Myths, legends, and stories often address the journey. Joseph Campbell spoke of the hero's adventure or journey. There are different types of journeys. Sometimes one is lured or wanders off on a journey. One may be go off into the forest and make a discovery that is valuable to mankind. Other times one intentionally sets out on a journey to slay the dragon that is threatening the people. Upon accomplishing the task, he returns as a hero. One may go on a journey in search of the Holy Grail.

At the individual level each of us confronts life's journey. The transition from the mother's womb into the world where the infant must begin breathing oneself is part of the journey. The transition from childhood to adulthood is part of the journey. Coming to know who we are is part of the journey. That is, discovering our calling, our purpose, or what Joseph Campbell called finding and "following one's bliss" is part of the journey.

Merely responding to the influences and forces of one's environment will not lead us to our dream. One may receive encouragement or support from others; however, the decision and journey to follow one's dream is up to the individual. No one can travel another's journey.

Is it always advisable to follow a dream? One must decide for one's self. Acting at the appropriate time is another important factor. At least in some instances, unless we follow our dreams, we do not discover abundant treasures meant for us.

Story 3: The Rosetta Stone

One of the great historic and archeological treasures of the world is the Rosetta Stone. Discovered in 1799 by French soldiers in Napoleon's army while in the Egyptian Nile delta near the city then known as Rosetta, the Rosetta Stone dates back to 196 B.C.E. Its use in 1799 was as a building stone. Along with his army, Napoleon had 167 scholars present in Egypt to collect artifacts. They gathered the stone for their collection. When the British defeated the French, the Rosetta Stone, along with many other artifacts, was ceded to the British by the Treaty of Alexandria in 1801. Since 1802, the British Museum has displayed the stone. It contains an inscription from a council of priests communicating their solidarity with the king of Egypt, Ptolemy V, and honors the deeds that the Pharaoh had done for the priests and people of Egypt.

The fact that it was used as a building stone is not what made the Rosetta Stone valuable. The fact that it contains an historical inscription praising the Pharaoh is important but is not what made it such a treasure. The stone contains an inscription written in two languages, Greek and Egyptian, and in three scripts— Greek, Egyptian hieroglyphic, and another less formal Egyptian script for daily use. Egyptians used hieroglyphic script for 3500 years— beginning in 3300 B.C.E. Before the discovery of the Rosetta Stone modern scholars did not know how to decipher Egyptian hieroglyphics though many had tried for hundreds of years. By comparing the Greek and less formal texts with the hieroglyphic text, the stone was vital in learning how to translate hieroglyphics. Jean-Francois Champollion received credit for translating the text.

Comments:

There are several intriguing features about the story of the Rosetta Stone. Foremost, what made the stone such a treasure was that it unlocked the secret of reading hieroglyphics. Reading hieroglyphics in turn opened the door for scholars to the study of the ancient Egyptian civilization— reading other hieroglyphic writings.

The purpose of engraving the stone was to communicate a message. That was the purpose served by creating the stone. Often the value or use of something evolves in an unpredictable manner. The priests who created the stone did not intend to use it to translate a dead language.

Often with new inventions, people have little or no idea of their use in future decades. The newly invented airplane was mostly for sport. It proved that man could fly. The military initially rejected its use, then they eventually realized that it was useful for surveillance. Now it has evolved into an essential armament. When the personal computer was invented, people were perplexed as to how it might be useful. They had no idea of its potential. Who could predict the rapid evolution of the personal computer?

The initial intended use of Coca Cola was medicinal, not a soft drink. Petroleum was first valued for medicinal purposes and then as an oil, kerosene, for lighting.

In addition, the Rosetta Stone is a story of potential. I wonder if some people are functioning at the stone level when they could be functioning at the inscription level or at the inscription level when they could be opening the door to new discoveries. Is there a potential theoretical physicist, another Einstein, somewhere working as a patent clerk? Every being has potential. Some have more than others do, some in one area, some in another. In *Man for Himself*, Erich Fromm said, "Man's main task in life is to give birth to himself, to become what he potentially is."

It is also significant that the Rosetta Stone was discovered. Historians believe that there were other stones with identical inscriptions placed at other temples throughout Egypt. However, no other stone has been unearthed. Not only did they make the discovery, but also the finding occurred accidentally. No one was intentionally looking for it. Happily, when the French found it, they did recognize and appreciate it for its potential value, even before they knew the reason. Those who recognize and appreciate who or what possesses value provide a great service.

Another lesson from the Rosetta Stone is that time and place matter. The Rosetta Stone was of far greater value in 1800 C.E. than it was in 196 B.C.E. That which is considered worthless at one time and place, may have enormous value at another time or place. What may not be valued now may be in the future. The story raises the question: How can people know what will be valuable in the future? Albert Einstein emphasized, "Try not to become a man of success, but to become a man of value."

Story: 4 Shakespeare's New Place

In Stratford-upon-Avon, William Shakespeare's hometown, there remains the house where his mother, Mary Arden, grew up and the house of his father, John Shakespeare. However, a garden grows on the spot where William Shakespeare's house, New Place, once stood.

Throughout its history, many highly celebrated figures visited Shakespeare's home. Hugh Clopton built New Place in 1483 and Shakespeare bought it in 1597. At the time, it was the only brick house in town. The author died there in 1616 and his wife Anne lived there until her death in 1623. Shakespeare's daughter, Susanna Hall inherited New Place who in turn left the house to her daughter Elizabeth Hall. Elizabeth married Thomas Nash who owned Nash's House, which is next door to New Place. Nash's House still stands and today serves as a museum whereby one may access the gardens where New Place stood.

Eventually, the Cloptons reclaimed New Place when Sir John Clopton bought it. He enjoyed opening his house to the public and encouraged tourists to visit. The citizens of Stratford were very proud of New Place, the home of the town's famous son. Tourists were eager to view the dwelling.

The happy story ends and an interesting segue begins with the next owner, Reverend Francis Gastrell. Gastrell, known for his cantankerous and eccentric nature, resented the citizens and tourists coming to sightsee. According to some sources, he first erected a wall around his property to obstruct the view of onlookers, although most sources do not mention the wall. People continued to come by and peek eagerly for a view. One night, in a fit of anger, The Reverend chopped down a mulberry tree in the garden that Shakespeare is believed to have planted. All he left was a pile of logs. Enraged citizens retaliated by breaking Gastrell's windows.

Gastrell had an ongoing feud with the city authorities as well. Since he was away from New Place much of the year, he did not believe that he should pay taxes on New Place for the time that he was out of town. The city authorities stood firm taking the position that since the house stood there all year, he should pay taxes for the entire year. The dispute went on and on and became more and more intense.

Finally, infuriated at the stream of onlookers and the tax matter, Gastrell demolished New Place around 1759. He destroyed the historical building so that only the foundation is visible. Incensed, the citizens of Stratford ran Gastrell out of town, threatening his life. Anyone with the name Gastrell was forever banned from living in Stratford-upon-Avon.

Comments:

In this story, nobody won. There were choices and challenges but everyone lost. The historically valuable house of one of the world's greatest literary figures was lost to posterity because of senseless wrangling. Gastrell destroyed his own valuable property. The Reverend taught the good citizens of Stratford a lesson though. He had probably warned them and he showed them, by golly. If calmer heads had prevailed, negotiation could have resolved the problem. Mediation did not exist as a formal discipline at that time but I am sure that mediators did and that there were citizens capable of mediating in Stratford. The Reverend did not engage his mind.

There were divergent expectations. The citizens were used to New Place being accessible. Apparently, the Reverend was used to his privacy. Psychotherapists learn that when one observes expressions of anger, that one should explore the hurt beneath, thus, embracing the heart. Each side became rigid and fixated upon their expectations and apparently did not consider the expectations of the other.

In addition, the story brings to mind the question: How will I be remembered? Will it be for destroying a valuable house or for building a house that will have significance in history or the history of someone's life? I would never have heard of Reverend Francis Gastrell if not for this story. I do not know anything else about him. He may have been a distinguished minister or scholar. He may have had good qualities that balanced his flaws. All I know is that he allowed his anger to destroy something that people treasured, something of great value. He lost perspective.

All of us have known this experience at some level. Distraction and annoyances can lead to so much anger that we lose perspective and fail to appreciate the value of what we possess. Sometimes we destroy treasures more valuable than an historical house. Sometimes we destroy relationships with children, siblings, friends, parents, and spouses. Sometimes we destroy ourselves.

Introducing Joha

Before proceeding, a character that plays a central role in many of the stories should be introduced. His name is Joha. Joha is a simple, good-natured, and likable man who came from humble origins. Although his line of thinking at times defies logic, he offers unique perspectives on situations and at times provides profound insights.

The character originated in the Middle East and is claimed by many countries. A few include: Turkey, Afghanistan, Iran, and Uzbekistan. He appears in various cultures by various names. Most authorities date him around the twelfth or thirteenth century; however, his life must have spanned several centuries based on some of the stories. For example, in some stories he travels by way of railroad train.

He is often known as Nasrudin and carries many variations in the spelling such as Nasreddin. At times, his name is preceded by titles such as Mullah and at times followed by titles signifying wisdom such as Hodja. Sometimes he is simply called Hodja. In China he is known as Afanti and in the Swahili culture as Abunuwasi.

I prefer the name Joha because I was first introduced to the character by that name. Besides, it is easier for me to spell and pronounce.

Story 5: The Perfect Mate

When Joha came of age to marry, he decided that he would go in search of the perfect wife. He carefully identified the qualities that he sought. Then he began his search. He attended all the social gatherings in surrounding villages and sought introductions as appropriate to the customs of his time and culture. The search continued year after year. Everyone that he met of marriageable age seemed to have some flaw that did not meet his criteria. He became frustrated but remained persistent.

At last, he met the perfect woman, one who met all of his standards. He was jubilant and announced to his family and friends that he was going to ask for her hand in marriage. As he left to make his proposal, he danced with joy. He observed the appropriate protocol and then it came time for him to pose the question. He told her of her great beauty, grace, and charm and then he asked for her hand in marriage. She paused and said, "I am flattered that you find me desirable as a wife. Thank you for your compliments. You, too, have many favorable qualities; however, I am seeking the perfect husband."

Comments:

Joha was not perfect but he was seeking perfection in a mate. Only those who are perfect have the right to expect perfection from others. Perfect spouses are scarce, but many imperfect partners can be treasured. Because someone is less than perfect does not mean that one may not be cherished and valued.

Those who are less than perfect have performed great human achievements. Great characters of faith were far less than perfect. The Hebrew pillars of faith, Moses and David, were less than perfect. Both were guilty of manslaughter or homicide.

On the other hand, since perfection is impossible, it does not justify one to use it as an excuse to wallow complacently in ineptness. Though unrealistic, in a sense it is commendable to seek perfection. Aspiring for perfection will not result in perfection but it may bring one much closer.

Abraham Lincoln said, “It is better only sometimes to be right, than at all times to be wrong.” The following quote is attributed to William Saroyan: “Every man in the world is better than someone else and not as good as someone else.”

Interestingly, there is another version to this story which presents a Zen student searching for a perfect master. He searched for twenty years meeting various masters but could not find the perfect one. Finally, he encountered a master whom he thought was perfect; however, when the student asked if the master would accept him, the master replied, “I only accept perfect students.”

Story 6: Happiness

Joha saw a man sitting dispiritedly by the side of the road. He asked the man what troubled him. The sad man said, "There is nothing of interest in life, my brother. I have sufficient capital that I do not have to work, and I am only on this trip in order to seek something more interesting and entertaining than I have in life. So far I haven't found it!"

Without another word, Joha seized the traveler’s knapsack and made off down the road, running like a rabbit. Since he was familiar with the countryside, he was easily able to out distance the traveler. The crooked road curved many times and Joha took shortcuts. He was well ahead of the traveler who followed the road. Joha placed the knapsack by the side of the road and waited for the distressed traveler. Following the winding road, soon the depressed man appeared, more miserable than ever because of his loss.

When he saw his property lying by the roadside, instantly his countenance changed. He ran toward it, waving, leaping, and shouting with joy. Joha laughed and said, "That is one way to create happiness."

Comments:

Rather than from time to time, but daily it is important to take inventory of that for which we have to be grateful. One of the simplest and most positively powerful forms of communication is expressing gratitude or writing a thank you note. Research indicates that gratitude is one important predictor of those who survive life crises and traumas. Grateful people are less likely to be depressed. Gratitude is a psychological survival skill. Seeking fulfillment and achievement in life are important, but a balanced appreciation for that which we already possess is important as well.

In addition, in taking inventory it is important for both individuals and organizations to recognize and appreciate the resources that they possess which are of value. What do I, or what do we, have to offer? What are my, or our, strengths?

As noted previously, in recent years, there has been greater emphasis in psychology on factors that contribute to mental well being rather than merely focusing on pathology or mental illness. Robert Emmons, author of *The Psychology of Gratitude* and editor of *Positive Psychology Journal* says that practicing gratitude can increase happiness by twenty-five percent.

In a 2007 interview, he reported that keeping a "gratitude journal" for three weeks can have positive lasting effects on mood for six months or more. His research also notes that practicing gratitude can have health benefits such as improving quantity and quality of sleep, increasing exercise, and fewer symptoms of pain. Dr. Emmons also notes that those who express gratitude "connect" better with others and are more optimistic regarding the future

Expressing gratitude is simple and a matter of common sense; however, having knowledge and acting upon it are very different. It is much more difficult for some than others to express gratitude. Hopefully, the traveler whom Joha encountered began to practice similar acts as those discussed by behavioral scientists.

In addition, research literature (Diener and Myers) points out the relationship between material wealth and happiness. People who live in wealthy nations are happier than are those in poor nations. However, after those in wealthy nations have enough to furnish basic needs, the relationship between material wealth and happiness declines. Also, study (Tim Kasser) has found that those who identify their goals in life as money, popularity, and image experience more negative emotions such as anxiety and depression and less satisfaction in life. G. K. Chesterton may have been commenting upon the traveler when he stated, "The way to love anything is to realize that it may be lost."

Story 7: Two Hundred Pounds

One of America's most substantive, renowned storytellers is Dr. Fred Craddock. Craddock told the story of a schoolmate who spent much of his life in China. He lived there with his wife and they had two children while in China. Eventually, the man and his wife were placed under house arrest by the Chinese government. Not knowing their fate, the family obviously experienced much anxiety. After a considerable time, a Chinese official came and announced that they would be released to return to the United States. As the family celebrated, the official stated, "You must pack quickly and leave with only two hundred pounds." They brought out their scales and began to decide what to pack. What clothes should we take? Which pieces of art should we pack? What books are most valuable?

After a while, the official returned and asked, "Are you finished packing?" "Yes," was the reply. "Does it weigh two hundred pounds or less?" asked the Chinese official. The Americans answered, "Yes." The next question was startling, "Have you weighed the children?" The couple looked at one another and then immediately began to toss out their most prized material possessions.

Comments:

Priorities matter. Treasure can turn to trash in an instant.

Conclusion: Chapter I

Some universities have a tradition called "The Last Lecture" in which periodically they invite seasoned professors to present what they would say if they had only one lecture left to deliver. When Professor Randy Pausch gave "The Last Lecture" at Carnegie Mellon University, it was different. With a diagnosis of pancreatic cancer, he knew that it truly was his last lecture. He spoke to a packed audience but the lecture was mostly for his three young children who would not remember what their dad had said. In his book, *The Last Lecture*, the professor presented himself as one who never lost the playfulness of a child combined with the effective, efficient thought of a scientist.

Dr. Pausch treasured possessing and fulfilling dreams. He believed that the parent's role is to teach children to enjoy life and "follow their own dreams." He said that parents cannot give children dreams or tell them how to find fulfillment in their personal lives, but parents can help by providing an environment that fosters and encourages children to discover paths that lead to dreams. As noted earlier, life obstacles often interfere with our discovering treasure. Pausch referred to obstacles as brick walls. He said that brick walls are there for us to see how badly we want something. Parents can help children learn to face and deal with brick walls.

Having a rooted faith in a system of meaning provides a reason to live. Friedrich Nietzsche said, "He who has a 'why' to live, can bear with almost any 'how'."

II: Touching and Transforming Relationships

1. **Pecan Trees**
2. **The Hand**
3. **The Tongue**
4. **The Samurai**
5. **The Cow**
6. **Heaven and Hell**
7. **The Merchant's Daughter**

Our relationships with others may create great happiness as well as great consternation in life. The following story serves as the introduction to Chapter II.

Story 1: Pecan Trees

Although all regions have them, one reason I enjoy living in the South is the opportunity to encounter interesting characters— fascinating, unconventional personalities. Felder Rushing is an example. He has his own way of living and looking at life. I do not know, but suspect that he may have acquired some of his qualities from his mother, Wilma Gene.

Felder advises residents throughout the nation but particularly in central Mississippi on botany and horticulture matters. He is a very interesting and popular speaker and people eagerly seek his advice when they have problems with their shrubs, trees or other plants or when trying to decide what to plant in their yards or gardens. The following is my version of a story reported in the *Clarion Ledger* newspaper.

Once on a radio talk program, he received a call from a grandfather who wanted to plant some pecan trees with his granddaughters and asked Felder for advice. Felder went into a spiel on all the problems with growing pecan trees and ended by throwing cold water on the project. Then the phone lit up with a call from Wilma Gene, who was not at all pleased with her son's advice to the previous caller. She said, "Son you blew it. You ruined everything. You missed the whole point." Felder asked his mother the reason she was so upset. She said, "That grandfather was planning a memorable experience that he and his grandchildren could share and cherish. That call was not about pecan trees; it was about relationships."

Comments:

The following stories are about relationships. They deal with ways of promoting relations as well as ways of resolving and dealing with interpersonal problems and conflicts.

Story 2: The Hand

A woman approached a wise cleric and stated that she was exasperated. She said that her husband was the stingiest man who ever lived and that he clung to every penny and could not turn loose of anything. The cleric said, "I will call on you and your husband tomorrow provided that it is agreeable with him." The husband sent word that it would be all right.

When the cleric arrived, the couple cordially greeted him and invited him to sit and have tea with them. They chatted for a while and eventually the subject turned to the issue at hand. The cleric asked them about their relationship and feelings for one another. Both agreed that they loved one another very much but that they had a serious conflict regarding money. The wife told of how stingy the husband was. The husband told of how impulsive and irresponsible his wife was with money. He said if she had a basket load of money, she would spend it all in one day.

After listening to both, the cleric raised his arm before them with his hand balled in a tight fist. He asked, "If my hand were always like this, what would you think?" They conferred and agreed that it would be deformed and not serve its purpose. Then he extended his hand so that his fingers were straight and rigid and held it before them. He asked, "If my hand were always like this, what would you think?" Again, they conferred and agreed that it would be of little use and deformed.

The cleric said, "If you know this much then you can live in harmony. There is a time to spend and a time to save." The cleric asked the couple to take one another by the hand. As they held hands the cleric said, "Go, teach and learn together and from one another."

Comments:

The cleric used a very simple metaphor symbolically to teach a difficult lesson. In so doing, it penetrated their rigid defenses and dispelled the spouses' anger. He could have advised them that they should unite and attack the problem rather than attack one another. That would have been good psychological advice but he did not choose that route. He chose a more indirect path. When hands are rigid, they do not serve their purpose or function well. When hands are flexible, they serve their purpose and function best. The same is true with partners.

Notice that the cleric did not suggest that the couple compromise. Compromise is one strategy but it is not always the best way to resolve relational problems. The compromising pose would mean holding the hand halfway between a clenched fist and a rigidly fixed extended position. That too would prevent the hand from being resilient, flexible, and serving its purpose effectively.

Furthermore, it is significant that though the spouses were at odds, each partner was willing to face and confront the problem. From my experience in couples therapy, the degree of commitment and motivation of the partners to resolve the problem, matters more than the size of the problem. Some couples break up over relatively minor issues while others resolve what may seem to be insurmountable problems. The cleric engaged the couple in working together, conferring about the meaning of the fist and extended hand.

A powerful predictor of success in any relationship is the realization that each can teach and each can learn from the other. Distinguishing when to teach and when to learn requires judgment as well. However, that is another matter.

Story 3: The Tongue

A Swahili story tells of a wealthy sultan who dearly loved his wife. She became ill and he anxiously watched as her health declined. She became more and more fragile. She grew listless and expressed no joy.

He called upon his chefs to try various diets that would help his wife gain weight and increase her energy level, but nothing they tried helped.

One day he noticed that one of his servants, a poor man, had a wife who was plump, full of life and vigor. He asked the servant, "Why is your wife so healthy and vibrant? What is your secret?" The servant said, "I feed her only the meat of the tongue."

Immediately the sultan ordered the chefs to gather the meat of the tongue of every animal they could find and prepare dishes for his wife. They prepared the tongue of every animal in the land but the sultan's wife continued to wither.

The sultan approached the servant again and informed him that his wife was continuing to deteriorate and the sultan was fearful that his wife might die. The sultan said that he must ask the servant to allow the sultan's wife and the servant's wife to exchange places. The sultan said, "I want you to take my wife to your dwelling and feed her the same way that you do your wife, and I will keep your wife."

The sultan's wife went to live with the servant and the servant's wife went to live with the sultan. (This is the ancient version of the modern television programs on swapping spouses.) After some time, the wives began to reverse courses. The servant's wife began to lose weight and became lifeless and the sultan's wife became more alert, energetic, and joyful.

When the sultan checked on his wife, he was very pleased with her appearance. He said, "I must know the secret of what the servant is feeding you." She said, "He feeds me the meat of the tongue; however, it is not the tongue of any animal. What vibrates from his tongue is the meat of poetry, stories, and music. This is what a woman needs to flourish."

Comments:

Jesus said, "Man does not live by bread alone." Neither did this woman. She could have anything that money could buy but that did not alleviate her depression. Like most of us, the sultan was successful and knowledgeable in some areas but not in others. He had accumulated great wealth and apparently could administer affairs of business but did not know how to nourish his wife emotionally. Though probably unable to transact business affairs effectively, the humble servant understood his wife's needs. The sultan was mature enough that he could learn from someone on a lower social level. It is interesting that the sultan learned from the servant rather than from his own wife. Did she understand her own needs or did the sultan fail to listen?

This story brings to mind the book, *His Needs, Her Needs* by Willard F. Harley, Jr. The author points out that what the wife prioritizes as important needs for her are usually different from what the husband prioritizes as his most important needs. For example, Dr. Harley states that women identify affection, conversation, and openness and honesty as the most important needs, while men list sexual fulfillment, recreational companionship, and an attractive spouse as most important. It is interesting to watch couples as they discover what one another value and need.

Drs. Gay and Kathlyn Hendricks discuss the importance of "the dance of individuation and unity" in relationships. Partners' need solitude, time to themselves, as well as intimacy and time together. Couples need to discover the right balance. They caution that the need for individuation and unity should be based in security. They note that some avoid intimacy because of anxiety or fear of rejection while others fear solitude and possess a need to cling and anxiety of being alone. Commitment leads to security so that partners may be authentic and self-disclosing and ask questions about what they do not understand as opposed to blaming and saying, "If I wasn't in this relationship, I wouldn't have this problem." The Hendricks state that partners may be together for thirty years and still lack genuine commitment.

The sultan and his wife seemed committed to their relationship. However, they lacked the intimacy to communicate authentically and effectively on the verbal level. Fortunately, perfection is not required to work through problems in relationships.

Diet is important. However, it did not serve as a solution for the sultan's wife. Nourishing words provide protein for the soul, just as meat provides nourishment for the body. The story suggests the importance of maintaining a balanced life. We need art (music, poetry, and stories) and intimate companionship as well as physical nourishment. It is important to work, but also to play and connect with others.

Story 4: The Samurai

A samurai served a very high official. He became very attracted to the official's wife and they had an affair. The official discovered the relationship and confronted the samurai. In self-defense, the samurai killed the official and ran away with the official's wife. They became wandering thieves going from province to province stealing and robbing. After a few years, the couple dissolved their relationship and went their separate ways. The samurai became tired of his depraved lifestyle and decided to atone for his behavior by devoting the remainder of his life to doing good deeds for others. He decided to search for something that he could do that would help others.

He found himself in a province where there was a dangerous road by the edge of a cliff. Many accidents occurred on the road. Numerous people had been injured and killed on the road that encircled the mountain. The samurai decided to dig a tunnel through the mountain to create a safe road.

He worked for twenty years digging the tunnel. Two years before the tunnel was completed, the son of the official whom the samurai had killed, found him and sought revenge. The son was an expert swordsman. The samurai said, "I will gladly give you my life but ask that you wait until I finish this tunnel." The official's son listened and agreed. After waiting a month, the son of the official grew impatient and asked if he could work with the samurai to complete the tunnel faster. The samurai agreed. After working with the samurai for a year, the son came to respect the samurai's strong will and character. He learned much from the samurai.

When the tunnel was completed and the samurai saw that the people could use it to travel safely, he said to the official's son, "Now that my work is done, you may have your revenge. You may sever my head." Tearfully, the official's son replied, "I cannot. You have opened my eyes to the true meaning of life and taught me much. How could I slay my mentor?"

Comments:

This is a story of personal transformation as well as relational transformation. Disenchanted with living selfishly and harming others, the samurai turned to selflessly serving others. Building the tunnel gave meaning and purpose to his life. Digging a road through a mountain, no small task, symbolized the journey from selfishness to selflessness. It was a huge undertaking. The tunnel connects. The samurai succeeded in digging a tunnel that saved others from danger and death.

Notice that the samurai did not rally the people of the region to join with him nor did he petition the governor to appoint a commission to conduct a tunnel feasibility study. He probably even neglected to fill out the appropriate forms or acquire a permit. He just decided that there was a job to be done and did it. What difference can one person make? What can a lone, individual do? Well, it depends. It depends on what one determines to do. Ask those who were served by Mother Teresa. Ask those who escaped Nazi tyranny by the leadership of Winston Churchill. Ask those who were led by Gandhi or Martin Luther King, Jr.

The samurai's attention focused on building a tunnel. He did not focus his attention upon himself. The only reason that he gave for sparing his life was to complete the tunnel. He was not trying to impress anyone nor was he trying to shape or influence the values, perceptions, attitudes, or behaviors of anyone. He was not trying, but he did. In fact, he impressed the man who hated him so much that he had devoted his life to searching for the samurai in order to kill him. The samurai impressed the official's son so much that it turned his life 180 degrees. That is what an individual who is selfless, determined, with a strong sense of purpose can do.

The official's son had no intention of changing. He was in a hurry to avenge his father's death so that he could get on with his life. He was blindsided. He did not know that when people work together toward a common goal that it transforms relationships.

Story 5: The Cow

According to *Psychotherapy Networker,* Milton Erickson was one of the ten most influential psychotherapists of the Twentieth Century. He frequently used stories and metaphors in his work. The first story of Dr. Erickson that I encountered was of Erickson as a boy living on a farm in Wisconsin. As I recall the story, he and his father were in the barnyard where the father was trying to drive a stubborn cow into the barn on a cold winter's day. The father started by trying to lead the cow; however, the cow refused to follow. Next, he went to the posterior end of the cow and slapped her on the behind a few times, but the cow would not budge. Then, he used his shoulder to try to push her from behind. The farmer pushed and pushed but the cow did not move toward the barn. Next, he went to the front and tried pulling the cow by the horns toward the barn. No matter how hard he pushed or pulled, the cow did not move forward. In fact, in the process, she even took several steps backward moving away from the barn.

Watching as his father become more and more frustrated and exhausted, young Milton said, "I believe that I can get that cow into the barn. Let me try." The father said, "Milton, you've seen how difficult my struggle has been and you are not nearly as strong as I. How do you think you can make that cow move? But if you believe that you can succeed, you are welcome to try." Milton walked over to the cow, took hold of her tail, and with all his might started pulling her backward away from the barn. As he pulled, she started walking forward and entered the barn.

Comments:

The story applies to both dealing with relationships as well as solving problems. First, it is necessary to accurately assess the situation or problem and understand the motivation. With whom and/or with what are we dealing? The Ericksons were dealing with a cow that was resistant and obstructionist. She was not motivated to cooperate; to the contrary, she was obstinate. The father and the cow were in a power struggle and the cow possessed greater power, at least physically.

Appealing to someone who is obstinate by the same means as someone who is cooperative is ineffective and can be very frustrating. Those who are cooperative will be more receptive to persuasion by dialogue. Dialogue does not usually persuade obstinate people. In fact, appealing to them with reason will probably reinforce their resolve to resist.

Young Erickson recognized what the elder Erickson did not. The father saw two alternatives: leading the cow into the barn or forcing the cow into the barn. The cow was unwilling to cooperate and the more force the father used the more resistant the cow became.

Young Milton recognized and used an alternative approach. He set up what is termed a "double-bind" situation for the cow. If the cow moved in the direction that young Erickson was pulling, that is, backwards, she would be cooperating with Erickson, thus failing to be resistant. She would be giving him control. If the cow resisted Erickson's pulling her away from the barn, it would result in the cow doing what Erickson wanted and she would go into the barn, which was in the cow's best interest in the first place. By encouraging and utilizing the cow's resistance, Erickson redefined the resistive behavior into cooperative behavior and cooperative behavior into resistive behavior. Redefining the meaning of behavior is one way to solve problems and resolve relational conflicts.

Football coaches often speak of the quarterback's skill to read the defense. A quarterback who is good at reading the opponent's defensive scheme can adapt and adjust his offense and employ offensive options that place the defense at a disadvantage. In dealing with interpersonal relationships, we need to read the strategies and motives of those whom we are encountering— not to defeat them, but to communicate on a meaningful level, which can result in building relationships.

The point is that in dealing with relationships, one will occasionally encounter oppositional behavior. I find this especially true in dealing with bureaucracies in government or large corporations. They often provide no way to communicate and no effective way to air complaints. Unfortunately, obstructionist corporate and government agencies are all too common. Organizations that genuinely desire customer feedback stand out.

To clarify resistance further, we may even encounter it intra-personally, that is within ourselves. For example, we may resist changing a bad habit such as adopting a more healthy diet. At times, a part of us may want to change but another part seems to obstruct change. If we experience resistance within ourselves, it is reasonable to assume that we will experience it interpersonally.

In interacting with others, it is unrealistic to assume that everyone will always be open to dialogue.

Often, we are not open to dialogue within ourselves. When encountering interpersonal resistance, we must first recognize it. Identifying resistance and accepting it for what it is can markedly reduce stress and confusion and place us in a better position to cope.

Story 6: Heaven and Hell

Once a believer approached a great prophet and inquired about heaven and hell. The prophet took the believer by the arm and led him through dark alleys and passages until they came to a palace.

They entered the portal and saw a large, striking banquet hall filled with all kinds of people. Some were rich and some were poor; some dressed in rags and some in jewels. In the middle of the hall was a huge bowl of soup sitting over a flaming fire. The aroma was pleasing. Each person had a large spoon as long as he or she was tall. The spoon bowl was made of metal and the handle of wood. The people were all emaciated, hollow-eyed, and frail. The closer they approached the soup pot, the louder and more rambunctious the behavior became. No one was able to manipulate the huge spoon to feed him or herself. Those who were strong enough to dip their spoons and lift them out filled with soup would spill it, scalding those around the pot. This behavior resulted in arguments, cursing, and fighting. The prophet said, "This is hell!"

The prophet took the believer by the arm and swiftly wisped out the door and through a dark passage into another banquet hall. The scene was the same in some ways but different in others. There was the large bowl of soup sitting over a fire. There was a hall filled with people of varying sizes, social classes, and types. Each had his or her soupspoon, which was the length of the person's height.

However, in this hall the people were well nourished and healthy in appearance. In addition, they were all working together in teams. One would hold the end of the handle while another held the handle nearer the spoon. They would dip the spoon into the soup and then lower the spoon so that the spoon's owner would sip until he or she was content. Then, they would change places and someone else would have his or her soup while others helped. The prophet said to the believer, "This is heaven!"

Comments:

The depiction of hell is as the eternal residence of those who are very selfish and have their own interests at heart. They operate rigidly in terms of their own regard without interest for the well-being of others. They may use others but those in the story did not trust one another, which was prudent. In hell, one takes advantage of another who is naïve enough to trust others. It is every man or woman for himself or herself. Thus, the interpersonal needs of everyone go unmet. Relationships are adversarial.

The depiction of heaven is as community—people work together in harmony, caring and sharing, giving and receiving. Heaven is a place where people work together and cooperate as a team. People are supportive, empathetic, and are aware of other's needs and concerns.

Those in hell had the same plenteous supply of resources, food, as those in heaven. The difference was their unwillingness to work together and share in order to utilize it. Working together to accomplish a goal is not always easy because by nature each of us has selfish tendencies. However, small acts of selflessness can produce major returns when it comes to building relationships and interpersonal transformation. President Reagan used to enjoy repeating the quote: "There is no limit to what can be accomplished, if you don't care who gets the credit." That is part of the difference in perspective between those in heaven and those in hell. Application of The Golden Rule is a foremost factor in differentiating heaven from hell.

Many great achievers recognize the importance of a famous quote by Sir Isaac Newton in which he said that any success that may be attributed to him was because he had seen further in that he had "stood on the shoulders of giants" such as Kepler and Galileo. All of us stand on the shoulders of others. From birth, our mothers nourish us and our families and communities socialize us. We learn to read, write and perform mathematical calculations because others teach us.

Neurosurgeons, who make many thousands of dollars per operation, invest great time and effort over many years learning their profession and developing their skills; however, others taught them the vast majority of what they know and what they can do. They deserve to be rewarded generously for their time and effort, but no matter how much they expend, they benefit significantly from the gifts of others.

Counselors and psychotherapists rely greatly upon the clinical innovations, theories, and research of those who preceded them. The same applies to other professions, trades, and occupations. Researchers, inventors, artists hone skills and share knowledge and procedures that they have received from others and develop them further. They pass information and skills to another generation. Teachers, whether formally or informally, play an important role in communicating crucial data.

While the initiative, responsibility, and hard work of the individual should be respected and applauded, we should not forget that we are all dependent upon others and one another. This does not mean that all are equally talented or achieve to the same degree. It does not mean that all should be rewarded equally. It means that those who recognize and appreciate our connectedness and interrelatedness are more prone to live as those in "heaven."

Story 7: The Merchant's Daughter

A wise king, whose subjects admired and respected him, administered the kingdom prudently. He enjoyed traveling about his realm consulting with administrators as well as those of humble status. Once while on a journey, he noticed a beautiful young woman who worked in her father's shop. The king found her so charming that he wanted her to come and serve in his palace. As was the custom of that culture and time, he approached her father, the merchant, and asked for his permission for the daughter to come to his palace. The king assured the father that she would be well cared for and secure. The father spoke with his daughter and told her of the opportunity and asked if she would like to serve in the palace. Without hesitating, she said, "Yes, I can think of no greater honor." The king arranged for her to come to the palace.

The king carefully observed the merchant's daughter as she carried out her responsibilities. He invited her to sit by him at the evening banquets. Soon he fell in love with her. Of course, there was the usual gossip about the appropriateness of the king's attraction to a subject of a lower social class. The king ignored any innuendos and looked for more opportunities to enjoy the company of the woman. He was so attracted to her that initially he failed to notice that she was becoming pale and losing weight. The longer she stayed at the palace, the more her health declined. When the king took notice, he called in the leading doctors of the kingdom but none could offer a cure.

Being a spiritual man, he prayed zealously for her well-being. One night after he had prayed fervently, he received a powerful vision in a dream that told him of a great healer who would come to the palace the next day. The dream instructed the king to follow the healer's directions. The next day the king was looking from atop his palace and saw a stranger approaching. He ran to greet him and asked, "Are you the healer?" The healer replied, "Yes, I am a healer. And you must be the king." The king extended his hospitality then eagerly took the visitor to examine the patient. The healer touched her forehead then checked her pulse for a long while. Then he asked to be alone with the patient.

He began to ask her questions about her home and family of origin. She began to open up and tell her story. As she spoke, she came to trust the healer and disclosed more and more. The woman told the healer more about her thoughts, feelings, and dreams each time they met. He asked if she had ever been in love and she said that she had. Then she told of an apprentice goldsmith who lived in her village. He was strong, handsome, and charming. She said that she loved him, thought of him often, and missed him dreadfully. She admitted that the opportunity to serve in the king's palace was such a great honor and rare opportunity that she believed at first that it was the best decision, but that she had now changed her mind. As she concluded telling her life story, the color began to reappear to her face and a slight sense of relief appeared. The healer told the woman not to worry and not to tell anyone of what they spoke.

The healer spoke with the king and asked of his feelings toward the patient. The king said that initially he was attracted to her by her beauty but had come to love her completely. He said, "I will do anything to restore her health." The healer asked if the king was sure that he loved the patient that deeply. The king gave his assurance. The healer then told the king that the only way to save the woman was to have the goldsmith from her hometown brought to the palace. Immediately, the king summoned guards and sent them with a sack of precious stones and carriage in which the goldsmith would ride. As the goldsmith entered the presence of the king and the healer, the healer called the goldsmith aside and inquired about his feelings for the merchant's daughter. He stated that he was still very much in love with her and missed her and could not feel attraction to anyone else.

Again, the healer called the king aside and in confidence said, "If you truly want this woman to be well, you must allow her to return to her village and marry this man, the apprentice goldsmith." The king's heart sank, he turned pale, and his eyes began to well with tears. He withdrew and said, "I never expected this form of cure. I must have time to think." The king retreated to a quiet place. He returned in less than an hour and said, "Though it grieves me deeply, if this is the only cure, let it be so!"

Comments:

The king wanted what was best for the woman he loved, even though it meant grief for him. In the end, true love overcame self-interest. The king faced and accepted his limits. No matter the amount of his power or wealth, he could not win her love. The king's love reflected shallowness as well as depth. No one loves perfectly or completely. Her physical beauty attracted the king initially, which is common. He thought he loved her before he actually knew her. He did not know what she loved. He did not know what was in her heart or mind. However, he did reflect maturity in that he did not use his power to control the woman he loved. He came to realize that sometimes loving means turning loose, letting go.

In addition, the king was willing to accept advice. Though others had failed at healing the woman, the king sensed the truthfulness of the advice of the healer. The advisor had the courage to confront the king with truth. That showed his courage. The healer served not only as a consultant but also as a wise mediator. He could have easily "botched" the dilemma if he had not been prudent and patient. He took his time and considered each person's feelings respectfully.

Another observation is that the wise healer knew that physical remedies could not cure all suffering. The woman's ailment involved "embracing the heart." The healer created an atmosphere and relationship where she could open up and tell her story. As the healer listened and established rapport, the woman came to trust him and became more self-disclosing. Each of us needs someone with whom we can open up to tell our story.

Research offers evidence of the healing power of self-disclosure. One good source is Dr. James Pennebaker's book, *Opening Up*. In addition, trauma therapy recognizes the value of having the victim go into explicit detail revealing thoughts, sounds, smells, and feelings. In *The Transparent Self,* Sidney Jourard said that dysfunctional people are those who have not made themselves "known to another human being and in consequence" do not know themselves.

Conclusion: Chapter II

One of the foremost qualities of psychological resilience is a strong healthy social support network. The resilient have close emotional bonds with others and work to develop close relationships characterized by authenticity, empathy, and genuine concern. Ideally, it is one's family. However, those who grow up in abusive or other types of dysfunctional families that offer no emotional support also exhibit psychological resilience. Often, they do so by distancing themselves, setting boundaries from their troubled families, and emotionally bonding and attaching to healthy friends and families.

Relationships play a vital role for those who survive extreme situations such as POW or concentration camps. Those in isolation go to great effort to develop tapping codes and other means of communicating to support and encourage one another.

III: Accepting Reality with Serenity

1. **The Flower Garden**
2. **The Mustard Seed**
3. **The Advisor**
4. **The Farmer's Horses**
5. **The Scorpion**
6. **The Fishing Trip**
7. **Day and Night**

The next two chapters, as well as the third, can be viewed from the perspective of the famous Serenity Prayer often attributed to the theologian Reinhold Niebuhr. Some attribute the prayer to others who predate him. The Serenity Prayer is commonly paraphrased: God grant me the serenity to accept what I cannot change, courage to change the things I can, and wisdom to know the difference.

Another perspective to view the next chapters is based upon a statement by Viktor Frankl in *The Will to Meaning* when discussing free will and determinism. He said that "man's freedom is not freedom from conditions" but instead, "freedom to take a stand on whatever conditions might confront him."

A third viewpoint is the common metaphor of comparing life to the card game, poker. Josh Billings said, “Life consists not in holding good cards, but in playing well those you do hold.” There is a time to hold, a time to fold, and a time leave the game as well as a time to flee. The successful gambler or survivor is one who knows when to do each. The metaphor is expressed poignantly by songwriter Don Schlitz in the song, *The Gambler*, sung by Kenny Rogers.

If one prefers Mother Goose’s “take,” there is a rhyme from several centuries ago that applies.

For every ailment under the sun
There is a remedy, or there is none;
If there is one, try to find it;
If there is none, never mind it.

One essential ingredient to effective living is accepting reality— what is. No matter where we are going, we must begin where we are, accept where we are. Carl Jung said, “We cannot change anything until we accept it.” Accepting reality connects with living in the present. What is, is; one must just accept it.

Psychotherapists often make a distinction between intellectual and emotional acceptance. Both are key ingredients but intellectual acceptance usually precedes emotional acceptance by a significant amount of time. Much of psychotherapy deals with emotional acceptance. When people deal with losses, such as physical disabilities or loss of loved ones, they may know that they will never be able to return to their former state and have accepted the event mentally. Yet, they may not have accepted it at the emotional level or in their hearts. They may feel frustrated, angry, and depressed. They may feel a loss of meaning, purpose, and worth. While accepting reality, changing what you can, and having the wisdom to know the difference are all vital to effective psychological survival, often they are not easily or clearly differentiated. The stories in this chapter are primarily about accepting reality both in the heart and the mind.

Story 1: The Flower Garden

Once upon a time, Joha decided to plant a beautiful flower garden. He searched and found the most colorful and attractive flowers available. He planted his garden and watered and cared for it daily. As his garden grew, he noticed that it was filled mostly with dandelions rather than flowers. He tilled and replanted the garden and again his garden was filled with dandelions. He repeated the process several times but always with the same results— dandelions! He consulted the horticulturists in his village and they offered their best advice. However, each time he planted the garden, he kept growing dandelions.

Finally, in desperation he sought out the chief horticulturist of the royal family. He consulted and received the most current, expert advice of the day. Joha carefully followed the advice of the chief expert but was dismayed when his garden produced the same results as before. Eventually, the chief horticulturist said to Joha, “I have given you the best advice known. I would suggest that you learn to appreciate dandelions.”

Comments:

Joha should be respected and admired for his persistence and determination, both at replanting his garden and obtaining the best advice available. Persistence is a positive quality common to achievers. However, after someone such as Joha has done the very best that he could, it was time to accept reality. Sometimes we must learn to appreciate dandelions.

Two additional points should be made. Acceptance does not necessarily mean forgetting or quitting. It means resolve. A possible solution may appear in time. In addition, psychological acceptance should not to be confused with someone who does not want to be bothered and passively "dumps" responsibility onto others. That is a manipulative way of avoiding problems or work. Avoiding or denial of reality should not be confused with accepting reality.

In this story, Joha was very industrious. He took responsibility and did the very best he could.

Story 2: The Mustard Seed

A woman who lived alone with her only daughter found her child stricken with illness. She called upon all the local medical experts of the day but none could help. After some time, the daughter, whom the mother cherished more than her own life, died. Grieved and desperate, she carried her dead daughter to a shaman who lived in the region. She asked him to bring her daughter back to life. The shaman said that he would try but that it would require a special ingredient to make a potion. The mother said that she would find the ingredient no matter how difficult. The shaman stated, "You must bring me a mustard seed." The woman said, "A mustard seed?" Why, that will be easy." The shaman added, "I need a special mustard seed. The potion that I must prepare requires a mustard seed from a home in a village that has not experienced death."

The woman began her search going from house to house. After having knocked on the door to the first house and having received a mustard seed, she asked the follow-up question, "Has there been a death in your house, your family?" The person said, "Yes, as a matter of fact we lost our parents. One died ten years ago and the other three years ago." She went to the next village and approached a house. She asked the woman who answered the door if she had a mustard seed and then asked, "Have you known death in your house?" The woman replied, "Unfortunately, I have. My husband died six months ago."

The mother continued for weeks and months going from village to village and house to house and found no one in a home who had not experienced death. Finally, after realizing the futility of her search she faced the reality that it was impossible to find a home that had not been touched by death. She realized that death is as common as mustard seeds. The woman returned home to face her loss and to begin her grief process.

Comments:

The death of a child is especially tragic. It does not follow the natural sequential order of life. A young mother is not as prepared to face and deal with the death of a child as she would be of an elderly mother or grandmother.

However, death is a part of life and is as inevitable as life. It may sound insensitive to say, but our fear of death indicates that we have not yet accepted our mortality. Of course, being able to accept one's death is an ideal, and few fully accept it until near the end of life. Paradoxically, we do not fully know life until we realize that we are mortal. All of us will inevitably die, that is, our physical selves will perish and life, at least as we know it, will end.

One may view this morbidly or be energized and invigorated to live life more fully. It may give greater purpose and meaning to live each day and experience each moment more abundantly. Once we fully come to accept our own mortality, the better prepared we are to live.

Also, realizing the transient nature of life is something someone has to come to know from one's own experience. It would probably have been futile for the shaman to explain to the mother that she must accept her daughter's death. But he could help her learn to accept death and he did. He helped her learn by inviting her to know of others' experiences. Knowing that others have shared similar events can be comforting and can facilitate acceptance. Support groups serve as an example.

Though a universal occurrence, for most personal mortality is the greatest experience that must be accepted. Joan Borysenko said, "The question is not whether we will die, but how we will live."

Story 3: The Advisor

A king who ruled a vast region always had his trusted advisor at his side. The minister was responsible and offered good advice but had a strange habit that annoyed the king. Whatever happened, the minister would say, "That is good. That is good." One year the crops in the kingdom were bountiful. The advisor said, "That is good. That is good." The next year there was a famine and the common people scarcely had enough to eat. The minister said, "That is good. That is good."

When the king confronted the apparent contradiction the minister explained that it is good to have plentiful crops so that people have enough to eat and they produce more and pay more taxes. On the other hand, he said that sometimes it is good to experience scarcity so people will learn discipline and be grateful for the years when crops are abundant.

One day the king was hunting. He sat atop his horse as he galloped along. Suddenly, the horse came upon a snake and threw the king to the ground. The king landed in an awkward position and seriously injured one of his toes so that it had to be amputated. In response the minister said, "That is good. That is good." In physical and emotional distress at his loss, the king became irate and ordered his advisor to be imprisoned. The minister said, "That is good. That is good."

A few months later, after he had recuperated, the king was out hunting again near the border of his kingdom when he became separated from his party. He happened upon a tribe of marauding barbarians who came into his realm to take what they might find. The king was captured and taken to the tribe's camp where they took his possessions and prepared to offer the king as a sacrifice to their gods. The king was tied to a tree while his captors sharpened their knifes and started a fire. As part of the ritual, the priest danced around the potential offering, inspecting the specimen to make sure that he had no blemishes and was a suitable sacrifice.

As the shaman examined the king, he noticed that there was a toe missing. He called the tribe around him and pointed out the flaw noting that he was an unfit offering. Since he was unworthy to be sacrificed as an offering, the priest said that the only alternative was to free the king. The king scurried away and soon met his party as they were searching for him.

When he arrived at his palace the king remembered his confidant, the minister, and called for him to be released. The king told the minister what had happened and said, "You were correct. It was good that my toe had to be removed. But tell me this. When I ordered you to prison why did you say it was good?" The minister replied, "If I had not been imprisoned I would have been by your side. Since all of my body parts are intact, I would have been an acceptable offering. The king said, "That is good. That is good!"

Comments:

In this case, the advisor was correct and everything worked out for the best. He must have been a gifted seer. He was confident and optimistic that everything would work out for the best. However, I can appreciate the king's annoyance at the minister. Optimism that is substantive and reflects care and concern is very different from shallow, superficial optimism that denies and avoids reality and discounts the hardship or suffering of others. If saying, "That is good" is dismissive, then "that is not good."

The terms "optimistic bias" and "depressive realism" have emerged from psychological studies. Results show that under certain important conditions depressed people are more accurate in assessing their ability to control reality than are those who are not depressed. Non-depressed or those with an "optimistic bias" may tend to overestimate their ability to control reality and thus devalue accepting reality.

I do not know of outstanding coaches or successful executives who are superficially optimistic. They may have high energy levels and be determined to encourage their team or organization, but they also have to think of positive and negative outcomes of decisions. Having vision and thinking of possible outcomes are important as well. Effective leaders must accept reality and have a vision of possible results.

Traditional Eastern and Western thinking differ in many ways. Eastern thought tends to emphasize that we are born into a world of suffering and in life we strive to deal with it. Western thought tends to emphasize that we should be happy and that anything that interferes with happiness is a problem. These are different views that affect our acceptance of reality. At first glance, Eastern thought may appear pessimistic and Western thought optimistic. However, is that the case?

If people assume that they are "entitled" to happiness, what happens when they encounter obstacles? They often become angry or depressed and generally experience negative emotions. "Why me? Everyone else is happy. I am entitled to the good life." On the other hand, if people accept that obstacles and suffering are part of life, they may be more appreciative of good fortune and feel blessed when they experience positive emotions such as joy.

Alan Watts wrote many books comparing Eastern and Western thought. One is entitled *The Wisdom of Insecurity*. He points out that life is insecure. If one ignores or fights insecurity, then one becomes more insecure. Paradoxically, if one accepts insecurity in heart and mind, then the person experiences greater security. Theodore Rubin pointed out that people facing problems is not the concern. He said that the true problem is to believe that life does not present obstacles and "thinking that having problems is a problem."

Story 4: The Farmer's Horse

A farmer's horse ran away. His neighbors were concerned and approached him and said, "That is terrible. What bad luck you have." The farmer said, "Good luck, bad luck. Who knows?" But his neighbors protested, "Without your horse you will have no way to plow your fields, harvest your crops, or pull your cart. You will starve." The farmer replied, "Good luck, bad luck. Who knows?" A few days later the horse returned along with several young horses. The neighbors came running and were excited. They said, "You are a blessed man. You have such good luck." The farmer responded, "Good luck, bad luck. Who knows?"

The farmer and his son left the horses in the field doing what horses do while the men built a new corral. In a couple weeks, they began to break the new horses. The son was thrown from a horse and broke his leg. It had to be set and he was unable to assist his father for several weeks. The neighbors gathered around again and said, "That is bad. What bad luck!" The farmer said, "Good luck, bad luck. Who knows?"

A week later a war broke out with a neighboring kingdom and all able-bodied young men were conscripted to serve in the king's army. When they came to recruit the farmer's son and saw his condition, they excused him from service. Again the neighbors gathered and said, "That is good. What good fortune you have." The farmer said, "Good luck, bad luck. Who knows?"

That night a lightning and thunder storm passed through and all the horses stampeded breaking and scattering the lumber of the new corral. The farmer had borrowed money to build the corral thinking that he would tame the horses and sell them for more than enough to pay for the expenses. That night the neighbors gathered again and said, "What bad luck! We can't believe that life is treating you so harshly." The farmer said, "Good luck, bad luck. Who knows?"

Next, the farmer planted his crops in the field that the horses had richly fertilized during their stay. Plentiful rain showers combined with interspersed days of bright sunshine resulted in an abundant crop. Upon seeing the fine crop the neighbors said, "You are so lucky to have such a crop. How fortunate you are!" The farmer said, "Good luck, bad luck. Who knows?" Then came time to reap the harvest....

Comments:

Who can say what will turn out to be fortuitous or unfortunate? The farmer was "laid back" and accepted what came. The neighbors who made value judgments upon what happened are the ones who vacillated. Agriculture is a vocation that is particularly dependent upon nature. The farmer plants, fertilizes, and cultivates but is dependent upon nature for rain and sun. Great teachers have used parables of sowing and reaping to teach lessons of spiritual significance.

One should plan and prepare for the future. It is foolish not to do so. One should also expect the unexpected. A thought expressed by the late psychotherapist, Dr. Albert Ellis, is that life is as it is and what is should be; it just may not be what we want or expect.

There is a saying, "Release the regrets of yesterday, refuse the fears of tomorrow and receive instead, the peace of today." (Anonymous) I believe that the quote best describes the farmer.

Story 5: The Scorpion

Once a student and his master sat by a riverbank enjoying nature. A scorpion moving by the edge of the river tumbled into the water. As the scorpion began to drown, the master reached into the water and saved the scorpion. In the process, the scorpion stung the teacher. The master and student sat quietly. Again, a few minutes later the scorpion began to crawl along the riverbank and fell into the water. A second time the master reached into the water and saved the scorpion. In course, the teacher was stung another time. The master sat patiently and poised by the river; however, the student became restless.

After the third time the scorpion fell into the river and the master was stung while rescuing the scorpion, the student could not restrain himself. He said, "Master, why do you continue to rescue that stupid animal and subject yourself to the poisonous sting. The master chuckled and replied, "It is the nature, or dharma, of the scorpion to sting. It is my dharma to save the scorpion."

Comments:

The master accepted the nature of the scorpion though it was the opposite of his. Though the term, dharma, is used in more than one way, it means to follow one's destiny and to evolve spiritually. Accepting someone with a different personality type or destiny in life reflects maturity. It is a part of the meaning of acceptance. While I would not equate psychology with religion or spirituality, most religious and spiritual viewpoints, as do most schools of thought in psychology, offer valuable insights. Appreciating and accepting the value of differences, without rigidly clinging to an extreme position reflects resilience which can bring wisdom.

Story 6: The Fishing Trip

A grandfather along with his son and grandson planned a weekend fishing trip. The grandfather had told his grandson fish tales since the lad could remember. The grandfather had taken his grandson, Throckmorton whose nickname was "Tadpole" or Tad for short, fishing several times at creeks and small lakes where they fished from the bank. This weekend was different. They were taking a boat and going to fish on a river.

Tad was so excited that he slept little the night before the trip. They left home before daylight and arrived at the river at dawn. Though gleeful, Tad began to experience some angst when he observed the swift flow of the river while Grandpa and Dad unloaded the boat. Tad's father helped him put on his lifejacket as Grandpa explained how deep the water was and the importance of wearing a lifejacket. Grandpa explained, "As long as you are wearing your lifejacket you will stay afloat if you happen to fall overboard." They launched the boat and steered upstream to one of Grandpa's favorite spots. Grandpa said, "I couldn't near about count all the fish that I've caught right here." Tad's father anchored the boat offshore.

Tad tried to practice the skills that his father and grandfather had taught him. He made cast after cast without a bite. After about thirty minutes, Tad made a cast and suddenly there was a strike. He held firm to his rod as he reeled in his first catch of the day. Dad and Grandpa were cheering and encouraging Tad. As he reeled the fish near the boat, Tad's father picked up the net to lean out to land the catch. However, the father stretched too far and fell into the river. Before Tad knew it, the current had carried his dad downstream far away from the boat. Tad shouted, "Dad, Dad, come back, swim as hard as you can!" To Tad's dismay, he noticed that his father was swimming farther and farther away from the boat. The father was not attempting to swim upstream toward the boat. Tad cried, "Grandpa, do something. Do something!"

The granddad placed his arm around Tad's shoulder and said, "Tad, I know that this is frightening to you, but it is not as dangerous as it seems. Your dad knows what he is doing. He swims well and has a strategy. You see, if your father had tried to swim against the flow of the river, he would become exhausted. That would be more dangerous than flowing with the current. Your father is a good swimmer and he is wearing a lifejacket. As he flows with the current, he will gradually guide himself toward the shore. We will raise the anchor and follow him downstream. When he reaches shore we will meet him. Events transpired as Grandpa had said. Tad was relieved.

Comments:

Tad learned an important life lesson that day. Learning can take place in a boat as it can in a classroom. This story segues into the next chapter. Tad's father accepted that he could not swim far against the current. He accepted reality by flowing with the stream. However, he was able to gradually steer himself to shore. He accepted reality by flowing and did what he could by steering or swimming to shore.

The story reminds me of the old Western movies that were popular when I was young. In those days often, there would be a scene where an attractive young rancher's daughter would be returning from town alone in a buckboard. The horse would "get spooked" and begin running out of control. The woman would lose hold of the reigns.

At a distance, a cowboy with the white hat and horse would observe the event. He would approach the buckboard from behind until he could catch up and overtake it. When he caught up with the horse pulling the carriage, he would leap from his horse onto the horse pulling the buckboard, grab hold of the reigns, and gradually bring the horse to a stop. If the cowboy had tried to stand in front of the runaway horse, he would probably be injured and the horse would continue running. By going along with the horse, he could more effectively bring it to a halt. Then the cowboy would see the woman home and meet the rancher. The rancher would tell the cowboy of a group of "bad guys" who were trying to take his ranch, which leads to a different story. The point is that sometimes it is necessary to go with the flow until the time and opportunity are available to instigate change.

Story 7: Day and Night

A Native American story tells of when the Cherokee people were new upon the earth. In the beginning, there was the daily cycle of day and night. The people began to discuss the day/night cycle and decided that life would be much better if it were daylight all the time— if there were no night. They pleaded with the Creator for constant daylight. The Creator heard their request and granted it. At first, the people were pleased. They could spend their time more actively. However, after a week they noticed changes in behavior. They became irritable and had difficulty sleeping. It was hot all the time and they missed viewing the sunrise and sunset. They missed relaxing in the coolness of the evening and hearing the sounds of the night.

The people met again, discussed the matter, and concluded that they had made a mistake. The Cherokee people missed the night and believed that they would enjoy night more than day. They beseeched the Creator for continuous night. The Creator granted their request. Again, at first they were happy. They enjoyed the relief from the heat and listening to the sounds of the night. They caught up on missed sleep.

After the first week, they began to become disgruntled again and by the end of the month were distressed. They missed the daylight. They tended to withdraw and felt melancholic. Their corn and herbs stopped growing. Fishing was very difficult in the dark. They tripped and stumbled as they maneuvered through the forests. It was cold and they spent much time gathering firewood. Some of the more feeble even died from injury or lack of nourishment.

The Cherokee people decided to call another meeting. They yearned for the way that it was in the beginning when there was a cycle of light and darkness. Humbly, they sought the Creator again. The people realized their mistake and reverently asked for the restoration of day and night as in the beginning. Once more, the Creator granted their request. The Creator told them that the creation of the universe follows the rule of pairs. Day and night, female and male, and birth and death serve as examples.

The people became content again. The weather was more pleasant. Their corn grew. Game was plentiful. Those who were ill recovered. The people were grateful to the Creator for both light and darkness, day and night. They offered songs of praise.

The Creator was sorry for those who perished during the period of darkness. In their memory, He placed their spirits in a young cedar tree. The cedar tree was to serve the Cherokee people as a symbol to remember their ancestors who died because of the extended period of darkness and as a reminder of the rule of pairs— the day/night cycle.

The Cherokee people respectfully accepted the symbol. The people made ornaments such as bracelets and necklaces of cedar. They treasured objects made of cedar and viewed them as bringing good fortune.

Comments:

What Cherokees learned from experience, modern science explains factually. The term circadian rhythm means "approximately one day" or about a twenty-four hour cycle. Circadian rhythms influence the biochemical, physiological, and behavioral processes of all living beings. Light/dark cycles serve as cues that affect "our biological clocks." The center in the brain that controls the biological clock is located very near the point where the optic nerves cross. The biological clock is sensitive to the conductivity of the optic nerves and light/dark variations.

Application of research varying the light/dark cycle has significantly benefited astronauts in space travel. Research continues to seek answers to problems related to shift work and jetlag.

An observation from the story that struck me was that while knowing that the people were making a mistake, the Creator was open to the requests of the people. The Cherokee seemed earnest and were eager to do what they thought best but openly admitted to their folly as well. The Creator allowed them to learn for themselves by granting their requests but was also sensitive to those who expired during the period of darkness.

As a result, He offered a symbolic reminder. The Cherokee people readily accepted cedar as a symbol. The wood in their ceremonial drums was cedar. They wore ornaments of cedar to remind them of what they had learned and should remember. Symbols and rituals may serve important functions as reminders. Is it not similar to the symbol of the rainbow that Yahweh offered Noah to remind people that He would not destroy the world again with a great flood?

The Cherokee story reminds us that since the beginning there has been ongoing change. There are cyclical, developmental, and evolutional changes. Change is inevitable. Psychologically accepting change is essential to living well. The Cherokee people learned that they lived best when they accepted the cycles of life.

Buddhists speak of *impermanence*. Impermanence means that everything is in constant change and nothing is the same from moment to moment. Buddhists acknowledge that change and impermanence may lead to suffering but without impermanence, there could be no happiness. A seed could not grow to produce fruit, which in turn produces more seed. A child could not grow into an adult and produce children who in turn reproduce another generation.

Thich Nhat Hanh advises the practice of impermanence, or using it as the object of meditation. Practicing impermanence will remove negative emotions, such as fear and anger, and open one to living in and accepting reality. As I understand it, he is saying that embracing impermanence goes hand in hand with spiritual growth.

The word "change" brings to mind an early memory: that of my paternal grandfather singing a favored song. He taught shaped note music and loved four-part harmony. He was born during the Civil War and his lifespan approached a century. I can still hear him singing, "Time is filled with swift transition.... Build your hopes on things eternal. Hold to God's unchanging hand." I have often thought of the changes that took place during the course of my grandfather's life. "Life is filled with swift transition." However, change seems to take place even more swiftly now. It seems that as much, if not more, change has occurred during the last fifty years than the prior hundred years.

Accepting change can be difficult; however, failure to accept change can be disastrous. One way to anchor life to survive the winds of change is to discover and serve a purpose that will extend beyond death. The father of American psychology, William James, stated, "The great use of life is to spend it for something that will outlast it."

Conclusion: Chapter III

Living well requires accepting reality, both in our hearts and minds. Change is inevitable and one must accept it. Alan Watts observed that trying to live without change is similar to "clinging to life" while holding one's breath. If you succeed, you die. Joseph Conrad advised, "Facing it— always facing it— that's the way to get through. Face it!"

While accepting change is vital to effective living, it also pays to realize that acceptance takes time; often, more time than others are willing to "accept." Accepting the death of a loved one or other loss, often takes longer than many realize.

IV. Choices: Changing What You Can

1. **City Gates**
2. **The Vizier and the Calf**
3. **The Turkey Prince**
4. **Lincoln's Depression**
5. **The Traveling Merchant**
6. **The Tailor**
7. **The Tea Cup**
8. **The Gingerbread Girl**

We do not have control over many life situations. We must accept certain circumstances. We cannot choose our parents, our race, or the time and conditions into which we are born. But we do have choices as to how we respond to those conditions.

The second part of The Serenity Prayer addresses the "courage to change what we can." Switching from prayer to poker, one must accept the hand dealt and play it the best one can. We cannot control the wind but we can control the setting of the sails and the rudder. The following stories deal with changing what we can in light of reality.

Story 1: City Gates

A wise, wealthy, and dedicated sultan was approached by a minister, a vizier, who had been traveling throughout the land. He said, "Most noble sultan, you have done so many great things for the people of the lands that you rule. In my travels to the cities, I encounter many who honor and appreciate you as their ruler, but there are others who laugh, sneer, and complain about you when I identify myself as your minister. You are a wise man. Please tell me why many do not appreciate your efforts."

The sultan said, "I have done my best to provide for the needs and development of the people. As you know, I have instituted an effective system of justice. I have built new roads to enhance travel and commerce. The roads connect the cities of the kingdom under my authority. I have built great walls to defend the cities. In my heart I want what is best for the people."

The vizier said, "I know this to be true. You have done many great things. But why do some still express negative opinions of you?"

The sultan solemnly looked at the vizier and said, "I can order that walls be built to protect our cities. I can order the great gates to the cities opened or closed at my will. However, I cannot control the tongues of my subjects. I must not be distracted by the discontentment of some of my subjects, but rather direct my attention to doing what is best for the kingdom.

Comments:

The sultan offered a classic example of choice of focus. He chose to center his attention upon building the kingdom rather than being distracted or trying to please malcontents.

Of course, there are times when discontented subjects should be heard and their views taken into consideration. But this was not one of those times. The sultan had a greater calling to pursue. "Obstacles are those frightful things you see when you take your eyes off your goal." (Henry Ford)

Story 2: The Vizier and Calf

Once a sultan accompanied by his inner circle was watching a magician perform. The sultan was enthralled with the show and turned to his vizier and said, “God has blessed this man with the ability to perform miracles. Have you ever seen such a genie?” The minister replied, “Your highness, he is very talented and brilliantly skilled as a magician but he cannot perform miracles. His skill has come from long hours of practice.”

The sultan was insulted; his fun had been spoiled. He argued with the vizier until he worked himself into a rage. He screamed, “One either has a gift or does not. You have none. What did I ever see in you to appoint you as my minister? Away with you, away to the dungeon! And so that you won’t be lonely, I am ordering that a calf be placed there as your cellmate. There you can speak with the calf about the skill and talent to practice magic.”

The vizier and the newly weened calf were thrown into the dungeon. The minister had always been an active, productive person and immediately set out on a mental journey to discover how he could use his time in prison productively. After thinking for a while, he lifted the calf to his shoulders and carried her to the top of the steps of the dungeon. Each day he repeated this exercise several times. As the calf grew, she rapidly gained weight.

After some months the sultan was working on a matter and remembered the minister whom he had sentenced to the dungeon. He called for the vizier and had him brought forth.

When the minister appeared, the sultan was amazed. He said, "What a miracle? What a genie? I have never seen such bulging, toned muscles." The minister left for a moment and returned carrying the calf that had been steadily growing. He said, "Your highness, no miracle has occurred. In your kindness you gave me this animal. Through my industriousness and practice, I have developed great strength."

Comments:

Again, we witness the theme of facing an obstacle and taking what control we have to grow, to develop potential. First, the minister had the courage to speak the truth to the sultan. He was polite and courteous but definitely not a "yes man." Answering the sultan's question forthrightly resulted in trouble as speaking truth often does. Speaking the truth does not always win out, at least in the short term. It is naïve to think that it does. However, people of character are called upon to speak the truth at times, regardless.

Also, note that the minister did not whine or become self-absorbed. He immediately went to work on another task. He looked in another direction, as if to the sea. He developed another part of himself, a part that he probably would have neglected had he stayed busy in the sultan's court.

I once heard a radio interview with a colleague of Albert Einstein. He said that the trait that amused him most about Einstein was that after he had completed a series of experiments that turned out to be futile, the next morning Einstein would be back at work starting a new project as cheerfully as could be and as if nothing had gone wrong. He was looking forward.

Miracles may sometimes occur. But that does not mean that we should passively wait for them when we can be actively productive in developing various aspects of ourselves.

(Note: A newborn calf may weight 70 to 100 pounds and a yearling may weigh 700 to 900 pounds.)

Story 3: The Turkey Prince

Once a prince of a great kingdom fell ill. As his condition deteriorated he came to think that he was a turkey. The prince removed his clothes and strutted around flapping his arms as though they were wings. He refused to eat at the royal table and ate the crumbs and scraps off the floor. This grieved and embarrassed the king deeply for the king loved his son. The king called all the great healers and wise advisors who tried to convince the prince that he was not a turkey; however, none succeeded. In fact the more they tried to convince him that he was human, the more the prince insisted that he was a turkey.

A stranger traveling through the kingdom heard of the prince's bizarre behavior and offered his assistance to the court. The king was desperate and received the stranger for an audience. The stranger said, "I believe that I can help your son." Ordinarily the king would have been more cautious and prudent but he was desperate. The stranger said, "I must move in and spend my days and evenings with your son." The king accepted the offer.

Upon meeting the son, the stranger disrobed and began to behave as a turkey. During the royal feasts he would sit under the table with the prince and gobble and eat the crumbs and scraps that fell. During the day they would strut through the courtyard and royal grounds. As they romped and frolicked together they became friends. After a while, the prince developed respect for the stranger and became receptive to his suggestions.

Upon winning the the respect of the prince, the stranger said, "I've been thinking. We belong to a proud and noble species. I believe that we deserve better treatment. Why are we sitting under the table eating crumbs off the floor when the royal court is eating from fine china? I believe that we should demand some plates and bowls." The prince said, "Yes, I agree with you. We are a dignified animal and deserve respect." They demanded plates and bowls and received them.

A few days later the stranger said, "I've been thinking more. Now that we have this fine china why are we eating crumbs when everyone else is served generous portions of gourmet food?" Again, the prince agreed and they began to eat their generous portions of food served on china as they sat under the table. After they were used to having the food served, the stranger said, "I've been pondering our situation more and something bothers me. We are clever animals and have much wisdom to offer humans. Why are we isolating ourselves and depriving them of our companionship and wisdom?" The prince said, "I will demand that we be seated at the king's table." The request was granted and the prince continued to recuperate until he reassumed his identity and role as prince.

Comments:

Please indulge me, but I cannot resist the moral: If you are going to be a turkey, strive to be a royal turkey.

The healer accepted the prince and his aberrant behavior. He did not try to talk the prince into changing. He did not criticize or ridicule the prince. He established rapport and then trust. The time to suggest change in a relationship is after trust has been established. The "stranger" never told the prince that he was not a turkey. Rather, he appealed to the noble qualities of the prestigous bird. Usually it takes time and patience to build a relationship of trust and respect from which change may occur.

Story 4: Lincoln's Depression

Numerous Lincoln historians have observed the significant presence of depression in Abraham Lincoln's life. At the time Lincoln lived, the term melancholy referred to a predisposition or tendency to develop what we would now call clinical depression and which they referred to as melancholia. A melancholy temperament did not mean that one would necessarily develop melancholia, which was considered an illness. Melancholy referred to a predisposition. A melancholy temperament also had positive implications in that it predisposed one to sensitivity, depth, and creativity.

There are numerous quotes both from Lincoln and those who were close to him that referred to a melancholy temperament as well as episodes of depression, especially during his early adulthood. There appears to be ample evidence of episodes to meet the criteria of what today is referred to as Major Depressive Disorder.

In a letter to his first law partner in 1841 he wrote, "I am the most miserable man living." He went on to say that if his depression could be distributed to the entirety of humanity that there would not be a "cheerful face" in the world. He added, "I must die or be better...." A portrait artist, Francis Carpenter, said that Lincoln had the saddest face that he had ever painted.

William Herndon, his third law partner, said that "melancholy dripped from him" and "The perpetual look of sadness was his most prominent feature." In confidence, Lincoln told Robert L. Wilson with whom he served in the Illinois legislature that he never carried a pocketknife for fear of what he might do.

During his twenties he lived in New Salem, Illinois. There are several citations of suicidal watches by friends and neighbors. Citizens would take turns sitting with him for days, believing that he was suicidal based upon statements that Lincoln had made.

From his childhood he was observed to have episodes of withdrawal and avoidance of others and he would not read or study for days, which was most unusual for him. He was observed to be sensitive and to have a strong desire to learn though he only attended school for about eighteen months.

From whence did Lincoln's depression come? No one can offer a definitive answer. Heredity may have played a role. Several of his relatives were noted to experience "blue episodes." Further, his childhood presented many traumas even for the times in which he lived. A brother died at an early age. His mother died when he was nine years of age. Near the same time he lost an uncle and aunt.

Lincoln's father returned to Kentucky in pursuit of a wife and left Abe and his sister alone for an extended period. There was significant conflict between Lincoln and his father. Abe was driven to learn and read at every opportunity at the expense of engaging in physical labor. His father considered Abe to be lazy.

The estrangement grew to the extent that Thomas, Abe's father, never met his son's wife or children. A. Lincoln did not visit his father when dying nor attend his funeral. That is a powerful witness to their relationship. Lincoln's sister, to whom he was close, died in childbirth when Lincoln was eighteen years old.

Furthermore, there was turmoil, both blessings and curses, in dealing with his wife, Mary Todd Lincoln. In addition, there were the deaths of his sons with which to cope.

From these inauspicious beginnings came a man who served one term, two years, in Washington D.C. in the U. S. House of Representatives and was later elected president of the United States of America during one of the most turbulent times in U. S. history.

Comments:

By today's standards many would expect that Lincoln's early life experiences would have resulted in his becoming a "victim" and "traumatized" and one who could never succeed in life. He would be considered prone to addiction or one unable to control his anger and rage because of life trauma. Today, some might insist upon institutionalization, perhaps in a forensic unit, where he could be psychologically evaluated to determine if he was a threat to himself or others.

However for some reason, instead of becoming a "prisoner" Lincoln became a president.

In addition, today he could and likely would be admitted to a psychiatric hospital and afterward spend his life under the care of mental health professionals. He would be told, "You have a chemical imbalance and must stay on psychotropic medications for the remainder of your life." However, instead of becoming a patient he became a president.

Joshua Shenk wrote a very interesting and inspirational book on Lincoln's depression, *Lincoln's Melancholy: How Depression Challenged a President and Fueled His Greatness.* Some might wonder how a book detailing one's depression would be inspirational; however, as one who has struggled with depression since early life, I found his battle, not only to survive but to thrive, very encouraging and uplifting.

Many are uncomfortable discussing depression or being in the presence of those who are depressed. Some even prefer to deny the existence of depression and offer trite recommendations or solutions to depression. The advice often stems from the advisor's anxiety and usually further alienates the depressed person. Some assume that anyone who is depressed is merely engaging in self-pity, which is sometimes the case and should be considered; however, that does not address the major condition of depression.

Those who are severely depressed can be difficult to deal with; however, those who struggle with issues of depression who are striving to survive and even thrive can be rewarding to work with in a therapeutic setting. Depression is often cyclical and one can be most supportive by accepting the other's depression and letting them know that they care. Rather than offering a "quick fix," recognizing, facing, and admitting one's anxiety about another's depression can be more productive for both parties. Many prone to depression are often sensitive and are talented and creative. The sensitivity that engenders their depression also seems to promote their productivity.

Fred Kaplan has written a book entitled, *Lincoln: The Biography of a Writer.* He argues that Lincoln, the man, cannot be understood without understanding Lincoln, the writer. He contends that Lincoln was a writer and examines his poetry, essays, and speech writing. Kaplan investigates the evolution of A. Lincoln's writing and compares it to Lincoln as a leader and a politician.

Several other authors come to mind in considering depression and creative writing. They include Ernest Hemingway and Sylvia Plath. Nell Casey edited the book, *Unholy Ghosts: Writers on Depression,* which include chapters by William Styron and, interestingly, Joshua Shenk discussing their depression.

Shenk examined Lincoln's life in depth and identified three stages. The first extended through early adulthood. It was a period of self-discovery and self-disclosure. Lincoln was driven to learn and absorbed as much as he could. Also, he experienced bouts of sadness and withdrew at times. He came to realize that his temperament was one of melancholy. Shenk noted at least two "breakdowns." There were times when Lincoln desperately sought relief and spoke of suicide.

One interesting quality in Lincoln during the first stage is that he did not, and perhaps could not, hide his anguish and despair. The absence of allusions to Lincoln judging himself negatively, or discounting or deriding himself, is significant. In one quote, he referred to depression as "a misfortune, not a fault." He gained insight through self-examination. After leaving home he found friends in New Salem who not only tolerated, but also seemed to accept him and express empathy. Shenk notes that in spite of Lincoln's depression, people were drawn to him. In my opinion, there is a difference between feeling or experiencing one's depression and using one's depression. Many who are genuinely depressed do not spread emotional misery to others, while some seem contagious.

Realizing that he would likely always possess a temperament susceptible to depression, Lincoln developed strategies for coping. He wrote and memorized poetry that helped him express his feelings. He collected jokes, quotes, and anecdotal stories. The biographer noted that Lincoln not only told stories and jokes that were entertaining to others but that he laughed heartily when he told them. Some believe that laughter even without humor is effective and promotes health. Thus, the second stage involved a strategy for coping.

The third aspect of Lincoln's life is that he believed that he had a sense of destiny or purpose in life. Though he was not religious in the traditional sense, he did reflect a depth of spirituality and "knew" that he lived for a reason. He told others that he believed that he had a sense of destiny, although I would doubt that he could specifically identify what it was or could verbalize it clearly until he was in his fifties. It turned out to be abolishing slavery and preserving the union.

I see many people who are facing physical and mental disabilities. Feelings of self-worth or value are often based upon what people can achieve physically.

Facing the loss of vitality to be active is frequently accompanied by depression. Those who adapt best to losses of ability to engage in activities that used to bring pleasure and satisfaction are those who come to accept the loss and then find new avenues to meaning and purpose in life. It takes time to accept losses and search to find other ways to discover fulfillment in life.

In spite of tendencies toward depression, Lincoln believed that his life had a purpose. I suspect that as he came to believe more and more that his life had a sense of purpose or destiny that his depression became more manageable.

Secondary sources report that Lincoln offered several suggestions for dealing with depression. They include taking a walk or ride with your spouse, wrestling with your children, laughing at your blunders, discovering "meaningful goals," sharing your aspirations with others, and developing friendships. He went on to say that if these recommendations do not prove helpful, commit to resolving a major "national dilemma."

From a psychological standpoint such suggestions would well apply to those with mild or initial states of depression but not to those who are severely depressed. I find it unusual that someone who experienced the depth of depression that Lincoln had known would offer such recommendations, but perhaps he did.

Lincoln had a predisposition toward depression. He accepted and dealt with it the best that he could by changing what he could.

The following quotes attributed to Lincoln offer insight into his resilience: "Always bear in mind that your own resolution to succeed is more important than any other" and "Die when I may, I want it said by those who knew me best that I always plucked a thistle and planted a flower where I thought a flower would grow."

Story 5: The Traveling Merchant

A traveling merchant would load his wares in his coach and travel the country selling his merchandise. He would leave his family and home town and be away for several weeks at a time and then return home, rest, restock, and go on the road again. Once while the merchant was returning from an extended trip having sold all his merchandise for a handsome profit, a robber leaped from the roadside hedges brandishing a hand gun and stopped the merchant's coach. The robber demanded, "Give me all your money or I will take your life." The merchant said, "You may take all that I have but please have mercy and don't harm me."

As he handed the thief the money the merchant inquired, "May I ask a favor? I have been away from my hometown for many weeks. When I return without any money, everyone will think that I am a complete failure. No one will believe me when I tell them I was robbed.

Would you be so kind as to fire two bullets into the door of my coach? That will provide some evidence that I was robbed." The thief did as the merchant requested. "Now, kind sir," asked the merchant, "I know it may seem ridiculous to you, but if you wouldn't mind, I'd like to remove my hat; if you would fire a couple of shots in it, that would be even more convincing." Again the thief was accommodating.

As the thief turned to leave, the businessman asked, "If I might impose to make one more request I promise this will be the last. If you would come closer and let me take off my coat and hold it away while you shoot some bullets in it, then I would be most appreciative." When the thief complied the merchant realized that the gun was empty and threw his coat over the head of the thief, overpowered him, and retrieved his money and sped away.

Comments:

Moral: If one is a thief, it does not pay to be accommodating.

As with the story of the vizer and calf, the character found a clever solution to his dilemma. The thief complied with the requests of the frightened victim who appeared powerless but in reality took control. As the thief went along with the merchant's requests, he depleted the resources that made him a threat. The victim took control by engaging the thief and led him down a path of distraction and then surprised him to retrieve his money when the thief lost his power to intimidate.

Story 6: The Tailor

A Jewish tailor moved to a different town and established a new shop. Another businessman in town who was antisemitic passed by and noticed the new shop. As he walked farther, he came upon some young ruffians who were skipping school. He suggested that they go to the Jew's tailor shop and create a disturbance. They stood in the street in front of the tailor's shop and yelled, "Jew! Jew! Jew!" at the top of their lungs. The tailor started to go out and confront them but stopped himself realizing that he would be doing what they wanted and the prospects of their leaving would be slim.

Instead, he went out and thanked the boys for helping him advertise his new business. He said, "If you would be willing to accept a payment, I would like to reward each of you with a quarter, and if you are not too busy, I'd like to invite you back tomorrow." The boys accepted the money and left. The next day they returned and again yelled, "Jew, Jew, Jew!" After a while the tailor came out and thanked them and handed each a dime and invited them back the next day. The following day they returned and repeated the same procedure. After a while, the tailor came out and handed them each a nickle.

They began to grumble and complain asking, "What kind of deal is this? You started out giving us each a quarter and now all we receive is a meager nickel for the same work." The tailor said, "That's all I'm paying. You may come back tomorrow if you wish. It's up to you." The "tough guys" discussed the matter and decided to give it another try. After all, in those days a nickel had some worth.

The next day they appeared before the tailor's shop and yelled, "Jew, Jew, Jew!" As usual the tailor came out and thanked them and handed them each a penny. The boys were angry and objected. They said, "Look you have been cutting our pay every day. It is not worth the effort and time to come over here for a mere penny. If you don't raise our pay, don't expect us back."

The tailor said, "That's up to you. You will have to accept what I pay or else. It is your decision." The boys left and never returned.

Comments:

This story offers an example of reinterpreting intented behavior and similar to the psychological term "reframing"— changing the interpretation or meaning of a behavior. The boys came to insult the tailor. He went along with the boys and reinterpreted their jeering as providing a service to him and rewarded them. Instead of reinforcing behavior to increase its frequency, he gradually decreased the reinforcement to decrease the frequency. The boys changed their perception of the behavior from ridicule to providing a useful service.

Story 7: Tea Cup

A famous Zen master was noted for being very clever even as a boy. Once as a boy studying under his master, he dropped and broke a prized, antique tea cup that belonged to the master. As he heard the footsteps of his master approaching, he thought quickly of how he would present the news. Holding the broken pieces of the cup behind his back he asked his master, "Why is it necessary that people die?" The master replied, "It is part of the order of nature. Something is born; it lives out its life, and when its time has come, it dies."

The boy extended his hands with the broken pieces of the tea cup. He said, "The time for your tea cup to die has come."

Comments:

The tea cup had been broken. There was nothing to do about that. It must be accepted. However, the boy did have a choice as to how he would report the event.

He could have chosen to deny any knowledge of it. He could have blamed it on someone else. He could have hidden it and waited to see when the master would notice. He chose the honorable way of telling his master, but also chose a clever way to present the incident by inviting the master to wax eloquently about the nature of life and death before the student presented the news.

Story 8: The Gingerbread Girl

In the 1960's Betty Alice Erickson and her husband, David Elliott, decided to adopt a Vietnamese baby girl. They had two sons who were blond and blue-eyed as was their father. Betty Alice had fair complexion and blue eyes. Interracial adoptions were rare at the time and many were prejudiced against them. They named their daughter Kimberly; however, her grandfather, Milton Erickson, preferred to call her "The Gingerbread Girl."

Dr. Erickson anticipated that Kimberly would encounter rejection due to her distinctive features and skin color. He sent cards and letters addressed to his Gingerbread Girl.

Whenever the family visited Erickson, he made sure that there were gingerbread cookies on the table. Only the Gingerbread Girl could serve gingerbread cookies. In Erickson's home, it was a serious violation of social etiquette for anyone other than The Gingerbread Girl to serve gingerbread cookies. Kimberly was in charge of serving the cookies to her brothers, parents, and others. Kimberly's Aunt Roxanna made a gingerbread doll, which she presented to The Gingerbread Girl. When Kimberly became an U. S. citizen, Erickson sent her a card of congratulations noting that she was now "an American Gingerbread Girl."

Granddad would hold a gingerbread cookie next to Kimberly's arm and comment that the colors were indistinguishable. Kimberly told her brothers about conversations that she and her grandfather had about ginger. She told them that it was a very extraordinary spice and that cookies make of ginger were served only on special occasions.

When Kimberly entered kindergarten, her teacher was Hispanic. On the way home from her first day of school, the new student said to her mother, "I'm really lucky." Then Kimberly added, "I went up to my teacher and held my arm next to hers. I showed her that I was a Gingerbread Girl, too."

Comments:

Erickson could not change other's beliefs, or prejudices. He could not have a significant impact upon changing others perception. Attempting to do so would be a losing battle, at least in the short run. Neither could Erickson change the color of Kimberly's skin, even if he had wanted.

He did anticipate that Kimberly would encounter bigotry and probably discrimination. He approached the situation proactively. He could influence her ego-strength, self-image, and sense of worth; he could help her develop psychological resilience. Erickson could help shape her self-concept, which gave her the psychological strength to deal with adversity. Fortunately, Kimberly was receptive and perceived her skin color and physical features as special.

After reading the story in the book, *Hope & Resiliency,* I became a grandfather to a child of Mayan decent. His sisters' skin color is as fair as mine is, that is, as white as Bill Clinton's legs. Though societal attitudes are very different now from those of the 1960's, guess what the granddad brings his Gingerbread Grandson whenever "Papaw" visits?

Conclusion: Chapter IV

Living well requires focusing upon what one may change rather than bemoaning what one cannot change.

One may have very little control over what may be changed but resiliency requires that one look for opportunities, no matter how small, to take action.

At times people may only be able to change their perspective or attitude. An Aldous Huxley quote applies, "Experience is not what happens to you; it is what you do with what happens to you."

V: Judicious Decisions

1. **King Solomon**
2. **The Bride's Decision**
3. **The Patient and Doctor**
4. **The Farmer's Estate**
5. **The Cookbook**
6. **The Hayloft**
7. **Posterity**

Chapter V deals with stories of decision making. How could one count the number of decisions one makes in a day much less a decade or lifetime? Learning to make effective decisions profoundly affects the quality and experiences of life. At times, decisions or solutions are obvious but difficult to implement. At other times, decisions or solutions are ambiguous and wise counsel is needed to untangle the intricacies. Discernment is crucial to making effective choices to challenges. A portion of The Serenity Prayer applies to the following stories. On occasion, the "wisdom to know the difference" may be more difficult than "accepting reality" or "changing what one can."

Story 1: King Solomon

Two prostitutes appeared before King Solomon (I Kings 3:16-28). One had given birth to a son three days before the other. They resided in the same house and no one else lived there. One night the mother of the younger child rolled over and lay on her son. When she awoke, the child was dead. Realizing that she had suffocated her son, she took the living baby of the other mother while his mother lay sleeping and replaced him with the dead son. When the mother of the living child awoke, she reached to caress her infant and to her horror sensed the coldness of death. She wept as the morning light grew brighter. She carefully examined the child and noticed that he was not her son but the son of the other woman. The women argued. Only the two women knew the truth, as there were no witnesses.

The real mother of the son approached the King and asked for justice. She told her story to the King. The mother who kidnapped the child argued profusely claiming the child as hers. The two women argued before the king until the matter was about to get out of hand. King Solomon intervened and said in essence, "Each of you says that the child is yours. I shall solve your dilemma." He then called for a sword and ordered, "Cut the child in two and give half to each mother." "No!" the mother cried. "Let the other woman have my son."

The mother was willing to allow a kidnapper to have her son rather than for him to be slain. However, the real decisive factor was that the mother of the deceased child was willing to allow the execution of the king's order. She said, "Neither you nor I will have a son." Then the text says that The King gave his ruling.

The one who resisted the slaying was the real mother. The King said, "Give the child to her."

The story does not end there. The record goes on to say that the people of Israel were in "awe" of The King when they recognized his ability to govern justly. As word spread, the king's decision communicated much to his subjects about their ruler.

Comments:

1. An authority figure acting as Solomon today would be sued, ostracized, defrocked, disbarred ... (at least in the USA). Justice requires boldness. 2. The mother had a combination of courage and compassion. Even though she was a prostitute, she did not hesitate to approach the king and was willing to sacrifice her son to a "Jezebel" to save his life. Though the son was too young to remember the event, he would always know of his mother's love for him. As we say back home, "That boy had a fine mama and I sure would be curious to know how he turned out." 3. The mother may have <u>been</u> a prostitute but I do not see a woman with her character <u>remaining</u> a prostitute. 4. Also, sometimes selfishness, cruelty, and anger absorb people to the extent that they unwittingly disclose the truth about themselves as did the mother of the deceased child. 5. In both women's cases, the "tragedy" revealed the true character of the person.

Story 2: The Bride's Decision

Once upon a time in an ancient land a wealthy official had a daughter who was strikingly beautiful and exceptionally bright. Many considered her the most charming woman in the land. Her mother died in childbirth and the daughter was raised by her father as the only child. In that culture, it was customary for the father to give his blessing before a daughter married. She had three suitors each of whom was responsible, gifted, and each seemed directed toward successful futures. Since the father would accept each suitor, he told his daughter to choose the man whom she would marry. The men competed intensely for her attention and affection.

Suddenly, one day she fell ill and ebbed in and out of consciousness. All were distressed. The most respected healers were consulted to examine the woman. They applied all the potions, remedies, and rituals that they knew, but none helped. Each gave a terminal prognosis. The father and the young men were united in their concern and sadness. The father was paralyzed with depression. One of the suitors assumed responsibility for caring for the father and his affairs. One left and traveled from country to country, seeking healing knowledge. The other suitor stayed by the bedside embraced the woman's hand and wept. He attempted to comfort her and attend to her every need. He decorated her room with flowers and prayed for her continually.

The one who traveled seeking knowledge found himself in a distant country with an unfamiliar culture. He heard of a healer who possessed uncommon knowledge and special powers. As he approached the woman's village, he found directions to the healer's residence. The traveler asked for an audience with the healer who hospitably received the suitor into her residence. As he entered her house, he noticed a vast array of herbs, flowers, and roots.

While they were sipping tea, the seeker explained the reason for his visit and described in detail what he knew of the woman's history and symptoms. In desperation, he pleaded for help. Upon finishing her tea, the healer closed her eyes and said, "I shall seek your solution." She appeared trance-like for minutes then began to direct the young man to select various items describing exactly where they were located on the shelves. Then she instructed him to grind and mix the plants into a potion and explained to him how to administer the concoction. As she opened her eyes and returned to her former state, she explained to the visitor that she had been blessed with a special gift of healing and did not fully understand it herself and had no memory of the instructions she gave. She then reassured him that if he would carry out the directions as given that she believed that the woman whom he loved would return to health.

Immediately, the suitor embarked on his long journey home. He traveled from dawn to dark. Upon arriving home, he went to the father's house where he found the father and other suitors. The one who had returned from the long journey told the others of his experience with the healer and showed them the potion.

The father questioned the seeker then asked him to administer the potion as directed. The suitor carefully dispensed the "prescription." Gradually, the young woman came to life. Upon recovering from their astonishment, the suitors rejoiced. However, after a while, they began to bicker and argue. The one who stayed by the bedside insisted that he deserved the woman's hand in marriage because he had felt her loss most deeply and demonstrated the greatest concern. The suitor who cared for the father and his affairs insisted that he deserved the bride because he had shown the most responsibility. The seeker argued that if it were not for him there would be no marriage, because he had searched the world for life-saving knowledge.

The young woman told the men to stop quarreling and that she would go away for a few days to a quiet place and make her decision. She appointed a time to meet with them to announce her decision and end the uncertainty.

At the appointed time, they met. She first spoke to the seeker and said, "You seek knowledge. I owe you the utmost gratitude. You are a great humanitarian and will be an outstanding benefactor to humankind." Then she spoke to the suitor who had cared for her father and said, "You have behaved as a dedicated son-in-law and have unselfishly served my father for which I am deeply appreciative. You will serve humankind commendably." She then addressed the suitor who stayed by her bedside and said, "While I am grateful to each of you and all of you have demonstrated great human qualities, I will receive your hand in marriage. I seek love most in marriage. You have shown me the most affection."

Comments:

The young woman confronted an approach-approach conflict in psychological terminology. A decision was required, but the options were positive. It was similar to choosing among scholarships to Princeton, Yale, and Harvard or winning a car and choosing among a Mercedes, Lexus, and Lincoln.

Did she make the correct decision? Which one should she have chosen? I am not a woman, and certainly not all women would make the same choice. I believe that I would have chosen the seeker. (Disclaimer: I should disclose that I am no longer married, which may suggest that I should defer in such matters of judgment.)

I hope that she made her decision maturely and wisely. I hope that the man knew the meaning of love and was truly devoted to her, rather than being overly sentimental or dependent. However, I must remember that co-dependency, enmeshment, and toxic relationships had not been "invented" at that time.

Perhaps I am the one who needs to learn from the woman's choice. Her choice was consistent with the generalization that most women place a high priority upon romance. It is consistent with Dr. Harley's list of women's needs (Chapter II) as well as the story in Chapter II, The Meat of the Tongue, where the sultan learned that his wife needed more than status, material possessions, and gourmet meals to flourish. The bride needed "the meat of the tongue."

Furthermore, the bride's decision is consistent with Bowlby's Attachment Theory, which emphasizes intimate emotional attachment and contact as the most basic, primary need. After World War II, John Bowlby, a British psychiatrist, observed that in crowded orphanages infants had low survival rates though they had all necessary physical needs met. He came to realize that babies need contact comfort, affection, and attachment to a loving mother or maternal substitute in order to survive and thrive.

In the last decade, Dr. Susan Johnson and others have studied Adult Attachment Theory and what she calls The New Science of Love. Her work is most impressive and complements and completes what is lacking in other theoretical approaches in psychology. Many psychotherapists view emotions as problems and discount them with terms such as codependence and enmeshment. Johnson believes that when you search beneath the surface levels of blaming, protest, and withdrawal that occur in couples' interactions, that each partner is seeking bonding, affection, and connection, that is, love. She uses the acronym, ARE. Partners seek significant others who are accessible, available and responsive or care about their emotional needs and who are emotionally engaged. Her approach is referred to as Emotionally Focused Therapy (EFT). EFT certainly seems consistent with the bride's choice.

Another mystery associated with the story is the role of the healer. She apparently went into a trance that transcended normal conscious awareness. It is reminiscent of the experiences of Edgar Casey who went to exceptional effort to scrupulously document his work and whose motives appeared most genuine.

Could it be that there are levels of consciousness that most of us are not aware of presently— levels that do not fit conveniently with our traditional "empirically based science?" Does integrity require openness to such a possibility? While many who claim to have special powers of healing are misguided or fraudulent and deserve censure, is it prudent today to adamantly insist that the healer was a fraud? In spite of the vast amount of information available today, there is still much that we do not know or understand.

Story 3: The Patient and the Doctor

Once there was an elderly woman who was almost blind. She consulted many doctors who told her that she had a serious eye disease. All of the physicians explained that the treatment would be very expensive and that they could not guarantee success. Though she lived modestly, she had inherited some expensive heirlooms. Valuing her vision more than her material possessions, she offered one of the doctors a large sum of money if he could restore her vision; however, if he could not restore her sight then she would owe him nothing. Several respectable citizens of the city witnessed the physician and patient's agreement.

The doctor administered treatment weekly. Initially the woman noticed nothing untoward and was hopeful; however, after a few weeks she observed that coinciding with each house call, one of her heirlooms was missing. One week a gold candle obera was missing; the next week a piece of china was missing; the next week a silver serving dish was missing. Upon his final visit, the doctor pronounced the woman cured. As the physician left, the woman could see nothing of value left in her room.

When the widow noticed that everything of value in her house was gone, she refused to pay the practitioner. After several confrontations, the doctor sued her for medical fees. When the woman appeared in court, she avowed that they had an agreement that she would pay the physician generously if he restored her vision. On the other hand, she would pay him nothing if he failed to cure her. As the judge questioned her, she astutely observed, "Before I was cured, I could see that my house was filled with vases, paintings, and china; however after the doctor pronounced me cured, I could see none of them."

Comments:

It is especially cruel to take advantage of those who are helpless, particularly with the pretense of helping them. The woman kept her composure. She was calm and self-assured. She did not present herself as a victim but assertively and cleverly made her point.

I would think that an honest judge would rule in her favor.

The story was adapted from one in *Aesop's Fables.* No moral appeared after the story. An old saying comes to mind that could serve as the moral: Don't p$$$ down my back and tell me that it's raining.

Story 4: Farmer's Estate

There is a traditional story of a prosperous farmer who died and bequeathed his land to his two sons. They tried to farm the land together but had problems. The brothers could not agree on anything. If one wanted to plant corn, the other wanted to plant wheat. If one wanted to raise cattle, the other wanted to raise swine.

Finally, they agreed on one matter; they should divide the farm and operate independently. There was an adequate amount of acreage so that each could make a respectable living even dividing the land into two farms, although it would substantially increase the overhead. The only problem was that they could not agree on how to divide the land. They would criticize and complain. One would suggest a way to divide the parcels and the other would scoff him and say that he was unfair. The younger would accuse the older of trying to take all the rich soil and the older would accuse the younger as trying to monopolize all the water resources. Their quarreling was childish and never ceased.

After years of wrangling and arguing, they decided to go to court. Each consulted a well-known, expensive attorney who told each what he wanted to hear. Each brother told relatives and neighbors his version of the conflict, which resulted in others taking sides.

The sons attended the same church, as had their father but their families would not sit on the same side of the sanctuary or one family would sit down stairs and the other in the balcony. Tension grew in the congregation. When the pastor heard that they were pursuing a court settlement, he sent word to each stating, "I want to meet with both of you tomorrow morning in my study." When the brothers met with the pastor, he asked, "Is it true that you are going to court to settle your differences regarding your father's estate?" Each "hemmed," "hawed," and finally mumbled, "Yes."

The pastor said, "Men this has gone far enough. We are strict Bible believers here at Antioch Church. You very well know that in I Corinthians 6:1-8, Paul implores church members to settle their differences within the church and not bring lawsuits against one another. Not only are you brothers in the church here at Antioch, but you are biological brothers as well." The clergyman surmised, "I have never been one to rank transgressions, but this one just might be of multiple proportions."

The pastor continued, "I am not Solomon, but I have a solution if the two of you are willing to cooperate." The brothers said, "Let's hear what you have in mind." The pastor said to the elder brother, "You divide the land into two equally fair parcels. Divide the land anyway that you want." Then he turned to the younger brother and said, "You have your choice as to which parcel you prefer." One brother said, "We've been arguing and arguing over how to divide the property and haven't agreed on anything." The cleric said, "This is different. This is the only way that I know of that you can agree on a fair settlement. Otherwise, I will suspect that you had rather argue than settle the matter."

Comments:

Each brother was given equal power. Each had to agree. Neither could take advantage of the other, unless the other was willing. The cleric offered an astute resolution to the problem. The wisdom to "know the difference" was available. What do you suppose the brothers did?

If the brothers truly wanted to solve the problem, a reasonable solution was before them. Those who genuinely seek solutions have open hearts and minds to recognize judicious choices. However, at times there are other deeper issues involved in disputes that have nothing to do with being rational or reasonable or seeking a solution. Special interests, personal schemes, and power struggles can interfere with solving problems. Presenting a judicious choice does not always guarantee that the parties will agree and make the decision.

Not only is willingness to resolve disputes important in disagreements between family members. It is relevant in business and customer relations as well as in dealing with differences regarding national and international matters. Competitive concerns and hidden agendas may sabotage decisions that offer excellent solutions.

Story 5: The Cookbook

The son of the founder of the Baha'i faith purportedly told the following story. While visiting in a distant city an elderly couple invited him to share their evening meal. As the woman anxiously went about preparing the meal, she took frequent breaks and left the kitchen and her cookbook. She went into another room to read from her prayer book. She trusted that prayers would result in the meal turning out especially well. Her strategy backfired and she ended up burning the main dish while praying. She apologized to the cleric and explained the reason that the dish had burned. He responded kindly suggesting, "It is good to read from your prayer book, but next time you are preparing a meal, I would propose that you stay in the kitchen and pray from your cookbook."

Comments:

At times, it is wise to wait patiently. However, there are also times to take action. The old adage is probably familiar, "God helps those who help themselves." Failure to take action created the dilemma. Divided attention or failure to focus upon a task can result in ambivalence and distraction. Distraction interfered with the cook preparing as good of a meal as she was capable.

Story 6: The Hayloft

In Lincoln folklore there is a story of Abraham Lincoln once winning a court case by simply telling a story and giving a one-sentence summation. He said, "Your Honor, the prosecution has the facts correct, but the conclusion is totally wrong."

Lincoln told the story of a farmer who had a young son and teenage daughter. The son came running into the house where his mother and father were talking. The boy was highly excited and short of breath. He sputtered, "Pa, Pa, come quickly. I just left the barn and saw the hired man in the hayloft with Sister. He has his pants unzipped and she has her skirt raised. They are about to pee on the hay." When the father returned from the barn, he said to his boy, "Son, you had your facts straight, but you reached the wrong conclusion."

Comments:

Judicious decisions require that one draw the correct conclusions from the facts. The couple in the hayloft was about to do something other than micturate on the hay.

Story 7: Posterity

Nationally recognized for leading the U.S. Senate Watergate hearings, the late Senator Sam Ervin, Jr. of North Carolina compiled many homespun anecdotes. In his book, *Humor of a Country Lawyer,* he tells interesting stories.

One story was of the time he arose to address the U. S. Senate to protest a spending bill. During a period of economic recession, the Senate voted on a spending bill that would raise the national debt. Also, they proposed a tax increase that would apparently pay little more than the interest of the increased debt. The tax increase would take effect in eighteen months, which was conveniently timed to be after the next election. The responsibility for funding the bill would fall primarily upon future generations. Those proposing the bill espoused the theory that the government should spend to stimulate the economy during periods of economic sluggishness and not raise taxes until the economy recovered. The basis for Ervin's argument was that it was "immoral" to increase the national debt and place the burden of payment upon our posterity.

The Senator then told an apocryphal story attributed to the British Parliament from the nineteenth century. A member of the House of Commons arose to propose issuance of a bond to pay for many temporary, "pork barrel," projects. There would be no payment on the principle for fifty years. Someone, who thought as Senator Ervin, protested based upon the argument of it being unfair to posterity. The member who proposed the bill replied that he did not care about posterity and that posterity had done nothing for him.

The spending bill passed despite Ervin's objections. Afterward Senator Russell Long of Louisiana commented upon Senator Ervin's address. In essence, Senator Long said, "Unfortunately, Senator Ervin failed to realize that posterity can't vote in the next election."

Comments:

"A politician thinks of the next election; a statesman [thinks] of the next generation." (James Freeman Clarke) At times, judicious decisions go unappreciated. Vision and concern for future generations led to Senator Ervin's decision; however, he lost the vote. Blame, attack, and accusations of improper motivation may result from a judicious decision. Integrity requires a person to maintain character and stand fast no matter whether others respond with approval or disapproval.

An outstanding example was Churchill's stance and warning of Nazi aggression throughout the 1930's. He saw the threat coming but was discounted and demeaned for speaking out. After the threat became clear, Churchill won election as Prime Minister and was given the responsibility to save democracy. After winning the war, Churchill chose to call for an election, based on his principles, though it was against the advice of his confidants who urged him to postpone the election for a year. Churchill lost the election in a landslide.

Voters carried placards exclaiming, "Cheer Churchill, Vote Labour!" It was not long before the British people needed Churchill again as prime minister and he served another term. Making and standing by judicious decisions overrides the capricious whims of others.

In World War II after the tide began to turn in the Allies favor, Churchill quibbled, "When I was called upon to be Prime Minister...there were not many applicants for the job. Since then, perhaps the market has improved."

Another observation that comes to mind from the story is the proliferation of programs and self-help books that boil down to saying, "Get out of debt and stay out of debt." I applaud those who offer the advice but find the widespread need appalling. As a nation, are we so illiterate and undisciplined when it comes to managing financial affairs? Are we economically and financially illiterate or addicted to instant gratification? Our politicians are atrocious role models. On last account, the United States was approaching ten-trillion dollars in debt and no doubt, the figure will be higher by the time you read this sentence. I shall refrain from going into a diatribe on the shenanigans that many get by with except to make one point; analyzing judicious decisions can elicit very strong emotions. Perhaps I should turn quickly to Chapter VII, Addressing Anger.

Conclusion: Chapter V

Judicious decisions require flexibility of thought, attitude, and viewpoint. Rigid thought or emotions deter problem solving and creativity. Resiliency requires examining obstacles from diverse levels, angles, and perspectives. Divergent and lateral thinking should be applied in addition to traditional logic.

VI: Stories of Folly

1. **The Rabbi at Lublin**
2. **The Practical Guru**
3. **Joha's Strength**
4. **The Lost Ticket**
5. **The Sage of Chelm**
6. **Chelm Justice**
7. **Joha and the Philosopher**

Ray Lum said, "You can change a mule but you can't change a fool." He may be correct but that does not mean that we may not sometimes learn from or be amused by folly. Just because we engage in acts of folly on occasion does not mean that we are fools. My friend and colleague, Dr. Waleed Salameh, advocates that each of us should allow ourselves a number of acts of "idiocy" each year; however, we should remember to set a quota.

One term may need clarification. Chelm is a legendary city in Jewish folklore known as the seat of foolishness. The people are affable and endearing but presented as befuddled simpletons. There is a city in eastern Poland near the Ukrainian border named

Chelm. Since we do not want to insult or stereotype the citizens of that city, for our purposes, we shall consider the names of the two cities as coincidental.

Story 1: The Rabbi of Lublin

The rabbi of Chelm went to visit a rabbi in the neighboring town of Lublin. Each rabbi was eager to impress the other with his acumen. The rabbi at Lublin presented a riddle. He asked, "Who is my father's son but is not my brother?" The rabbi from Chelm thought and pondered and pondered and thought. He discussed the matter over lunch and beseeched the rabbi of Lublin to give him hints; however, the host refused. Before the visitor left, the rabbi of Lublin gave the other rabbi the answer. With great pride in his accomplishment the host stated, "Me."

The rabbi from Chelm was impressed. He could hardly wait to get home and impress the congregation with his brilliance. At the next gathering, he arose and presented the riddle, "Who is my father's son and is not my brother?" The congregation was puzzled as had been their rabbi. They thought and thought and discussed the question. Finally, they gave up. At last, a spokesperson arose and stated, "We do not know who could be your father's son and is not your brother." With the confidence of a sage, the rabbi disclosed, "It's the rabbi at Lublin."

Comments:

An old Asian proverb says that those who know that they know and do are wise. They can teach. Those who know that they do not know can be taught. They are students. Those who know but do not know that they know are asleep. They should be awakened. The proverb does not address those who think that they know but do not. Perhaps they are foolish.

Story 2: The Practical Guru

An Indian student was zealously studying under the tutelage of his guru. Once the guru told him, “All is one; all is Brahman.” The young man became so excited with his newfound insight that he could not contain himself. He walked for miles through the streets repeating, “I am Brahman; I am God!” After a while, he met an elephant coming down the street. The mahout riding atop the elephant screamed, “Get out of the way; get away!” The student reasoned that since he was God and the elephant was God, why should he move aside? Meanwhile the mahout kept shouting, “Get out of the way! Get out of the way!” The student, still exhilarated, kept saying, “I am God. I am God.” Soon the decisive moment came. The elephant wrapped his trunk around the student and slung him to the side of the street. Stunned by the experience, the student gathered himself and realized that he had no major physical injuries, though he was scratched, bruised, and psychologically distraught. He immediately ran to his guru.

As he approached the guru, the student explained the occurrence and asked, “I am Brahman and the elephant is Brahman. In such an instance who should defer?” The guru asked, “How much does the elephant weigh? The student said, “I would estimate at least four tons. The guru then asked, “And how much do you weigh?” The student replied, “About 130 pounds.” The guru contemplated and answered, “It is true that all is one and all is Brahman, but in such an instance it would be prudent for the one who weighs four tons less to concede the right-of-way.”

Comments:

Actually, this version is not exactly the same as the one told by Joseph Campbell. Campbell said that the guru replied, "Why did you not listen to the Brahman shouting from atop the elephant?"

Story 3: Joha's Strength

Joha was sitting in a crowded coffee house with some friends when a noted philosopher entered. There were no other seats available; therefore, the sage asked if he could join Joha's circle. Joha was eager to speak with the wise man and was very pleased at the opportunity. Joha began questioning the renowned philosopher regarding his beliefs and philosophy of life. At first, the wise man sipped his beverage and was flattered by Joha's questions. As the philosopher continued to respond to Joha's questions, he became leery as to Joha's understanding of the philosopher's answers. The philosopher finished his drink and started to excuse himself.

Joha said that he wished to ask three more questions and then would ask no more. Joha inquired, "Are your beliefs now the same as they were ten years ago." The wise man replied, "Yes." Then Joha asked if his beliefs were the same as they were twenty years ago." The philosopher's reply was the same. Then Joha asked if his beliefs were the same now as thirty years ago. The sage replied stridently, "Yes, of course. Truth does not change. My philosophy is the same as it was ten, twenty, and thirty years ago." The philosopher then left.

A few weeks later, the philosopher needed someone to help him move some possessions. Joha's wife heard of the opportunity and passed the information to her husband. Joha had not worked for a few weeks and needed to earn some money. He went to the philosopher's house and asked for the job. The philosopher was skeptical and stated, "I am afraid that you could not handle the job. I need someone who is young and strong." Joha confidently assured the philosopher that he was as strong as he was twenty or thirty years ago." Eventually, Joha's confidence and persistence assuaged the reluctant philosopher. After all, the philosopher had insisted that his beliefs had not changed. The philosopher began by asking Joha to load some chairs onto a cart. Joha bounced back spryly and asked, "What's next?" The philosopher pointed and asked, "Do you see that large chest over there? That should be loaded next."

Joha approached the large chest and tried with all his might to lift it. He sighed, groaned, and grunted but the chest did not budge. Joha tried again but had no success. The philosopher turned to Joha and said, "I thought that you were as strong as you were thirty years ago." Without a pause Joha said, "I am. I couldn't have lifted it then either."

Comments:

Losing physical abilities is difficult to accept but losses associated with aging are inevitable. It is most unlikely that Joha could have been as strong as he was thirty years ago. Perhaps he was in denial. On the other hand, or simultaneously, he may have been using humor as an effective coping strategy.

Story 4: The Lost Ticket

Joha decided to take a trip to visit his uncle in a distant city. Joha rode his donkey to the train depot, bought a ticket, and boarded the train. The train was crowded and he could not find a seat, so he had to stand. When the conductor came by and asked for Joha's ticket, Joha started reaching in his pants pockets and then the pockets of his coat.

The conductor asked Joha to reach in the breast pocket of his shirt stating, "That is where most men keep their tickets." Beginning to panic, Joha kept re-checking the same pockets and even reached into the pockets of some people around him. The conductor became more insistent that Joha look in his shirt pocket. Joha said, "No. My shirt pocket is my last resort. If the ticket is not there, I would have no hope of finding it and would have to exit the train." Finally, Joha relented. He closed his eyes, gritted his teeth, reached into his shirt pocket, and handed the conductor the contents. Along with some papers, there was the ticket.

Comments:

Through folly, the story reflects a significant insight into human behavior. Most of us have experienced the fear of failure. One may believe that one has the talent to achieve but asks, "What if I fail? What if I attempt and fail as a performer, writer, or entrepreneur? What if I run for election and lose? Will people ridicule me?"

People who do not care about you probably will make disparaging remarks. However, if you have the talent and the desire is a priority, and then do not try; both you and those who do care about you will be disappointed.

One example is that of Clifford Kuhn who is a psychiatrist at the University of Louisville. Dr. Kuhn holds a special interest in the role of humor in coping and adapting to life stress. For instance, he has utilized humor, respectfully, in working with cancer patient groups.

For years, he had interest in standup comedy and wondered if he could perform on stage. When it came time for his sabbatical, he decided that it was time to try standup comedy. Though he had a career to rely upon as opposed to most performers, he risked professional derision. For the relatively short period, his effort was a success and he even worked as a warm-up act for some well-known performers. Though each can be rewarding, performing comedy is much different from teaching and clinical practice. In performing comedy, the audience is present to be entertained. Your jokes are accepted or rejected immediately and publicly. Dr. Kuhn took advantage of the opportunity to launch out, take a risk, and fulfilled an aspiration.

Confronting the fear of failure and taking risks to learn and to grow may involve either minor or major life decisions. Learning a language, learning to play a musical instrument, or practicing dietary self-discipline may represent relatively minor decisions but nonetheless bring a sense of accomplishment and result in self-growth. Decisions regarding career changes or where to live are major choices. Some choices fall between major and minor decisions. Even when we fail at something that we passionately aspire to, we learn—or at least should. Timing and other personal responsibilities should be taken into account, especially in making major life decisions that affect others. However, they should not be used as excuses that abort growth.

Joha was fearful of failing in a minor affair. Though fearful, Joha eventually mustered the courage to check his shirt pocket for the ticket. Interestingly, the ticket was located near Joha's heart. Literally, he touched his heart. Figuratively, one might surmise that one must embrace the heart to generate the courage to act.

Story 5: The Sage of Chelm

At a Chelm city council meeting, one of the members arose to make a motion. Since the city possessed so many citizens of "great wisdom," she emphasized that they should do something to commemorate and publicize the "fact." She explained that it would improve the morale of the citizens and promote tourism. Someone seconded the motion and the vote passed unanimously. Next, the question came as to how to remind the citizens and visitors of the cities' "reputation" as the seat of wisdom. The council discussed the matter until late night. The chairperson suggested that they go home, think about it, and discuss it at the next council meeting. The council adjourned.

At the next meeting one of the members suggested that the city should invite the citizens of Chelm to participate in a poll and rank the citizens based upon their wisdom. The person with the highest rating would be the chief sage. The motion passed. The citizens voted and elected a chief sage. After the election, the chief sage met with the city council and complained that as he moved about the city and traveled to adjoining communities that no one recognized him for his wisdom or sought his advice. People treated him as anyone else. "We must find some way that I am recognized," he asserted. The council agreed and decided to buy a pair of golden shoes for him to wear whereby he would be distinguished.

As the chief sage sported his new shoes through the streets, mud covered the shoes. No one could see the golden shoes. The council decided to solve the problem by buying him a pair of leather shoes to wear over his golden shoes and thereby protect the shoes of gold. The chief sage came back to the council complaining that while the leather shoes protected his golden shoes that no one could see the golden shoes.

The council called another session to solve the problem. A council member proposed a solution. He recommended that the chief sage wear the leather shoes on his feet and hold one of the golden shoes in each hand. “Hear, hear,” the council cried. The vote passed unanimously.

Comments:

In an effort to appear wise, one may appear foolish and pretentious. This is especially true when committees make decisions. Instead of developing their real strengths, they wanted to “reinvent” their public image concerning their weakness. Instead of striving to overcome their weakness, they elected to try to change public opinion. Organizations seem to often use the same strategy.

This story brings to mind our society’s tendency to rate or rank everything. Recognizing, rewarding, and promoting achievement is important and should be encouraged. However, ranking items, people or places in order from first to last often approaches the behavior of the council at Chelm. Though clearly there are measurable differences on dimensions involving people, places and performance, who can say who is the brightest, best dressed, or most outstanding person of the year?

Questions employed to identify opinions of where, who or what should be ranked to engage in interesting discussion or debate may be constructive. However, who has the right to draw definite conclusions on where the best or worst city to live is or what the best school or corporation is. If one considers specific favorable variables, almost everyone could find a way to be ranked high. Even when ranked by a single factor, the difference between number one and number ten may be miniscule.

There is an old saying that everyone wants to find someone on whom to look down. I like the response of an older fellow with whom I used to work in the summers whenever he heard the saying. He would add, "And if you can't find 'nobody' else, then help yourself to me."

By the way, if I were to rank the best city in which to reside, it would be the one where my grandchildren are located.

Story 6: Chelm Justice

The town cobbler in the city of Chelm was arrested for assualting a citizen. After hearing the case, the judge sentenced the cobbler to twenty years in prison. Upon hearing the verdict, a citizen of Chelm arose and pleaded, "Judge, you have sentenced the only cobbler in our town. To whom shall we turn to repair our shoes?" The other citizens agreed and asked the judge to consider the extenuating circumstances. The judge deliberated, then addressed the townspeople, "Citzens of Chelm, you have a good point. It would be a great disservice to the city to take away our only cobbler. Since there are two roofers in town, I will sentence one of them instead."

Comments:

I do believe that I can name some psychologists and bureaucrats who studied ethics and justice under the judge at Chelm.

Story 7: Joha and the Philosopher

Joha aspired to acquire great knowledge and wisdom. He thought and thought about what he could do. Finally, it dawned on him that one of the wisest philosophers in the region lived in a nearby village. He went to the village and inquired as to where the wise philosopher lived. Joha went to his home and beseeched him to share his wisdom with Joha. At first the sage said, "Away with you, I am a busy man and have no time for the likes of you." As Joha pleaded and persisted, the philosopher finally relented and said, "I will be passing through your village at noon next Tuesday. Tell me where you live and I will stop by and spend thirty minutes with you. That is all the time that I can spare." Joha was exhilarated. He gave directions to his house and excitedly ran home.

When the next Tuesday arrived, absentmindedly, Joha forgot about the appointment and went to the market to make some purchases. Upon arriving and finding no one home, the wise man became annoyed. He fumed and asked himself why a prestigious scholar would schedule an appointment with such a simpleton as Joha. In chalk, he wrote "Stupid Oaf" on Joha's door.

When Joha returned home, he saw the inscription. He said, "I have had a visitor. Who could it have been?" While examining the chalk inscription, Joha realized, "Oh my, it must have been the philosopher." After slapping himself on the forehead,

Joha immediately ran to the village where the philosopher resided and knocked on the door. When the philosopher appeared, Joha apologized and without thinking blurted, “When I returned home and looked at my door, at once I recognized your name and signature. I am so sorry for forgetting.”

Comments:

The philosopher’s hubris was exposed. Though he may have been naïve, Joha responded well. “Education should teach us to play the wise fool rather than turn us into the solemn ass.” (Kenneth E. Eble)

Conclusion: Chapter VI

The resilient do not pursue folly; however, they can recognize their folly and openly admit and learn from mistakes. Psychologically mature and secure people possess the capacity to laugh at themselves. “A man who knows he is a fool is not a great fool.” (Chuang-tse)

VII: Addressing Anger

1. **Cyrus**
2. **Gaius**
3. **Antigonus**
4. **Philip**
5. **The Buddha**
6. **Ray Lum**
7. **The Donkey**
8. **Henry Clay**
9. **Gettysburg Soldier**

We live in a culture that is becoming more and more uncivil and polarized. We engage more in quarreling and arguing to win what some call "debates" or "interviews." Too often, "winning" is more important than discovering facts or the truth. Character assassination has become a game. Deborah Tannen wrote a book entitled *The Argument Culture* in which she points out that our culture equates verbal attack with critical thinking.

The law of supply and demand may apply to attitudes and emotions as well as economics. Rancor and anger are in abundant supply. If one has doubt, attending to our media should suffice. Much of our comedy is aggressive and filled with disparaging remarks and insults, to say nothing of interviews and editorials involving politics and sports. The supply of civility seems limited. If one could trade civility on the commodity exchange, it should be selling at a premium. Its supply is scarce.

I remember the old public service radio message by Bill Cosby. Referring to driving too fast, he said, "Speed kills." Anger, too, can be deadly. Chronic anger can be destructive to the one who holds it as well as to the potential victim of expressed anger. On the other hand, anger can be constructively turned to advantage at times.

Organic or biochemical factors may contribute to anger. People may grow up in dysfunctional environments that may foster anger. Anger may be modeled in formative years and seen as the way to solve problems. People may learn to use anger to manipulate, intimidate, or control others. No matter the source, resiliency requires that people take responsibility for their anger and learn to deal with it.

Chapter VII presents ways of addressing anger and may apply to dealing with other negative emotions. Anger is representative of an emotion usually considered negative. Other negative emotions such as depression could have been discussed instead

Story 1: Cyrus

According to the ancient historian, Herodotus, in 539 B.C.E. Cyrus, King of Persia, hurriedly led his army to capture Babylon. When he approached the Gyndes River, which flows into the Tigris, he attempted to ford the river though the stream was swift and the undertaking was perilous. Though advised against it; nevertheless, Cyrus ordered his army to cross. In the process, one of his favorite royal white horses, used to pull the royal chariot, drowned.

Cyrus was enraged. He cursed, stomped, and raved. He was determined to seek revenge. Reportedly, he said that he would reduce the river to where women could cross it without raising their skirts. Though time was of the essence in preparing for battle, he had his army stop their drive and divert the river into 180 channels. The streams flowing in different directions left the river powerless.

Comments:

Cyrus "taught the insolent river a lesson" but in the process lost valuable time, much of the summer season, and was unprepared for battle. His army lost morale as well as respect for their leader and wasted much of the energy they needed for battle.

One attempt to explain anger is the frustration-aggression hypothesis, which was proposed, by Dollard and others in 1939. According to the hypothesis, aggression results when something or someone interferes or frustrates the achieving of or approaching a goal. The Ganges River interfered and frustrated Cyrus achieving his goal to reach Babylon. Thus, Cyrus responded with aggression.

Research that is more recent has suggested that the closer one is to achieving a goal the greater the likelihood of aggression. For example, Harris (1974) found that if a person is second in a grocery line and someone cuts in front, the person in line is more likely to respond with verbal aggression than if the person was tenth in line. In addition, the prospect of aggression relieving the frustration is a relevant factor. If acting aggressively is less likely to reduce frustration, then aggressive behavior is less likely. Also, Berkowitz emphasizes that not only is the internal state of frustration a factor but the presence of environmental cues or "aggressive cues" such as access to a gun may increase the probability of aggression. For example, Cyrus was in authority and had an army at his disposal.

While the frustration-aggression hypothesis is helpful in understanding anger as in Cyrus's case, it is not always applicable. Many social scientists view the frustration-aggression hypothesis as being overly simplistic. Anger or aggression may occur without frustration.

One may learn to use anger by observing role models during early development. Bosses, spouses, or children may use temper outbursts to manipulate or intimidate others in order to have their way. Sometimes people feign uncontrollable rage in an effort to be declared psychologically disabled and/or avoid legal repercussions.

Story 2: Gaius

In *On Anger, III,* the first century stoic philosopher Seneca told of Gaius Caesar, the adopted grandson of the Roman Emperor Augustus. Gaius razed a beautiful villa near Herculaneum. The reason for the act was that his mother had been imprisoned there at one time. Gaius had always sought revenge for his mother's imprisonment.

Before Gaius destroyed the villa, Seneca noted that as people traveled by, they admired the beautiful building. After Gaius destroyed the villa, people's curiosity was aroused as they passed. People asked, "Why was the beautiful villa destroyed?" By his very act, Gaius gave publicity to his mother's misfortune. Before his destructive act, few knew or were concerned about his mother's imprisonment. Afterward, word spread throughout the region and people wondered why she was imprisoned.

Comments:

The first two stories of this chapter provide examples of leaders consumed and controlled by anger, which turned out to be self-defeating and self-destructive. Their anger did not work to their best interest.

Seneca offers ancient advice on dealing with anger. 1. Lofty expectations, or what some call excessive optimism, can induce anger. When expectations fall short, then the disappointment can turn to rage. Such was the case with Cyrus. He held unrealistic expectations about crossing the river, though advisors warned him of the danger. Further, he expected nature not to defy him. Sports fans often have lofty expectations of their teams. When the team does not meet those expectations, they may demand that someone be fired. 2. Another is that vengeance exposes the seeker to danger and possible injury. To paraphrase Seneca: "Would anyone in his right mind try to repay a mule by kicking it or a dog by biting it." The mule and the dog are better at kicking and biting than humans are. He observed that often when one is successful in achieving vengeance and defeats the enemy, the victor sustains injuries and is left lame. The same would apply psychologically as well as physically.

3. Seneca recommends forsaking anger rather than waiting for anger to forsake you. Valuable time

and energy are wasted seeking vengeance. The time could be spent building friendships, reconciling with enemies, developing abilities, and serving causes in which one believes. 4. Also, Seneca observed that many grow angry out of envy. One may think, "I know more than those people. It is unfair for them to be so much more successful than I." Seneca noted that there are many below you who probably are having the same thoughts about you. He suggested acknowledging gratitude for the position that you do have combined with patience and using energy constructively. 5. In addition, Seneca points out that there are times to respect one's adversary. There are times when others fight for a cause with which we may disagree. He suggested respecting others who fight for their beliefs bravely and with valor even though their cause may differ from ours. 6. Seneca also proposed that anger could be relieved or avoided with mirth.

Story 3: Antigonus

Furthermore, Seneca provided examples of leaders who were provoked to anger but acted in their best interest by restraining from retaliating aggressively. The following two stories offer examples worthy of imitating.

When Antigonus's army was traveling, one night there were two soldiers standing very near their commander's tent. As subordinates are prone to do, the soldiers were complaining and expressing an unfavorable opinion of their leader and sharing opinions on how an army should be led. Antigonus clearly heard every word the men were saying since the only barrier between them was canvas. Instead of becoming angry or having the men punished, he understood that such behavior was common. He reached over, shook the tent, and said, "Move farther away. The General might hear you." Little did the soldiers know that it was the General who warned them.

On another occasion, Antigonus had his army traveling through a wet, swampy area on a very muddy road. Again, one night he heard soldiers standing outside his tent complaining of how difficult it was to march through the mire and how some of the soldiers sank to their waists. The next day Antigonus dressed in inconspicuous attire and went to the area where they were having the problem. There he found some of his soldiers stuck in the mud to the extent that they could not move. He waded in, extended an arm, and began rescuing the soldiers. When the soldiers were resting on solid ground, the General said, "You may curse Antigonus as much as you want for leading you into such a miserable swamp, but do not forget to bless the one who rescued you."

Comments:

Historians vary as to whom the stories should be attributed; at least it is a Macedonian named Antigonus, though Seneca and Plutarch seem to differ as to the identity of the person. For our purposes, it makes no difference.

Leaders are going to be criticized no matter what they do. Antigonus was able to accept criticism as a matter common to human behavior. He did not allow the behavior of his soldiers to provoke him to anger. He treated his army with respect. His attitude likely invited and instilled a desire in the soldiers to follow him when he led them into battle. In the latter case, Antigonus gained valuable information about the concerns of his troops. A good leader listens. A leader of lesser character would have acted aggressively and had the soldiers punished: an act which would demonstrate ruling by intimidation and fear.

Story 4: Philip

According to Seneca, Philip II king of Macedonia, who built his country into a powerful state, entertained a delegation of Athenians. He hosted them in royal fashion. He listened to their concerns. When it came time for their departure, Philip asked the delegation if he could do anything to address the needs and concerns of the people of Athens. A member of the envoy, Demochares Parrhesiastes, known for his insolence, stated, "Yes, you may hang yourself." (Following is my interpretation of Philip's reply.) At first, there was silence. The rest of the delegation was breathless and speechless. The Athenians then became incensed at the statement of their colleague and rebuked him for what they referred to as his "boldness."

Calmly and assertively, Philip turned to the rest of the delegation, excluding Demachares, and said, "When you return to Athens, please inform the citizens that it takes greater "boldness" and courage to restrain from assailing someone who makes a statement of great arrogance, than not."

Comments:

Philip made an outstanding point. It requires greater courage to restrain oneself than to act impulsively when angry. It requires greater strength of character to refrain from responding to an insult.

I believe that the delegation understood Philip's message, however. Philip did not act rashly or impetuously. The delegation was embarrassed and afraid and knew that their colleague was behaving disrespectfully which could well have ruined the purpose of their visit. Philip responded calmly and assertively. He did not respond to Demochares, or did he? He turned to those who were silent. He sent a clear message to the people of Athens: Demochares's attitude will not be tolerated when dealing with me. The next time we meet, send a diplomat. In the words of Ray Stevens in the song, The *Shriners' Convention*, he, Demochares, "had done embarrassed the whole Hahira (Athenian) delegation."

Seneca recommended that one way of dealing with anger when provoked was to look at the examples of those such as Antigonus and Philip and ask oneself, "Am I mightier than he?" Though they had great power, neither sought revenge in dealing with colleagues or allies.

Story 5: The Buddha

A seeker approached the Buddha and asked, "Is there anything that you would kill?" Buddha replied, "Yes, anger. Killing anger creates peace and relieves suffering. The wise know that killing anger removes anguish and brings contentment."

Impressed, the seeker decided to follow the Buddha and entered a monastery. The seeker's brother was irate when he learned that his brother had become a monk. He approached Buddha with great anger, cursing and swearing at Buddha. The Buddha remained calm and showed no discontentment as he smiled. Enraged the brother screamed, "Why don't you respond?" The Buddha said, "If someone offers a present and the other declines to accept it, then it must be taken back by the giver. Anger harms both the giver and receiver."

Comments:

Because someone else is angry does not mean that we have to respond with anger. Though tempting, if one yells a curse at me, I do not have to become angry and curse back.

Buddha refused to accept the "gift of anger." He realized that he had a choice. He challenged the giver. Thich Nhat Hanh speaks of the "seeds of anger" and the "roots of anger." He observed that when the seeds or roots of anger are present within a person, minor irritations can bring anger to the surface and result in expressions of rage. He recommends identifying any seeds of anger in oneself and replacing them with seeds of compassion, joy, and love.

Anger creates suffering in both the giver and receiver. Seeds of anger may be planted from childhood or social experiences and the carrier may or may not be aware of their growth. A biblical proverb reads, "A soft answer turneth away wrath:...." (Proverbs 15:1) A Chinese proverb states, "If you are patient in one moment of anger, you will escape a hundred days of sorrow." Ambrose Bierce is attributed as saying, "Speak when you are angry and you will make the best speech you will ever regret."

Story 6: Ray Lum

Ray Lum (1891-1976) was a mule and horse trader from Vicksburg, Mississippi who traveled throughout the South, Midwest, and West. Dr. Bill Ferris, former chairman of the National Endowment for the Humanities (NEH), wrote a book about Mr. Lum. It is entitled *You Live and Learn: Then You Die and Forget It All,* a saying which was one of Lum's favorites.

In his younger days, he would travel up to the Mississippi Delta to a place called Delta City to trade. The delta often lacked civility in those days. Lum believed that the reason that he escaped being assaulted was because of his frequent laughter and good sense of humor.

Lum kept his animals in a lot there in Delta City. A fellow by the name of Caney Bayou Smith came to town every day. He would "get liquored up," have two or three fights, and then stagger home. One morning when Lum was beginning to trade, Caney approached Lum and said, "I'm going to give you a good thrashing." The trader said, "Caney, I've been thinking about taking you on and I would love to whip you. You come back to the stock lot at six o'clock this evening and we will have a round. Nothing would please me more." Lum continued trading and Caney Bayou Smith drank all day and engaged in his customary fighting.

As instructed, Caney remembered his six o'clock appointment and arrived at the stock lot on time. Caney asked, "Are you ready to fight?" Lum said, "Caney, you wait right here. Don't go anywhere. I'm ready to fight you but I have to eat supper first." The mule trader left and returned in about an hour, after his meal. Caney was not anywhere around. Lum wondered if Caney became tired of waiting, passed out somewhere, found someone else to fight, or went home.

Comments:

This story reminds me of the old saying, "Don't kill someone who is busy committing suicide." Caney became more and more intoxicated and more worn from his other fights during the day, which was to Lum's advantage. Instead of striking while the iron was hot, Lum waited for the iron to cool. While "agreeing" with

Caney that they ought to fight, Lum took control of the interaction by setting and delaying the time for the fight. Being a rebellious sort, either consciously or unconsciously, Caney may have thought that he was not going to take orders from Lum.

There is an old saying that when you are angry that you should count to ten before you react. Another version may be to wait until after supper or around seven o'clock.

Story 7: The Donkey

One day Joha was out walking when he encountered a neighbor in the road who was enraged at his donkey. The neighbor was fuming, snorting, and cursing his donkey. As the neighbor shouted, stomped, and screamed, the donkey stood passively in silence. Joha approached his neighbor and asked what he was doing. The neighbor said, "I'm admonishing my stupid ass." Joha said, "Your 'stupid ass' will never understand what you are saying. You must learn to speak to your donkey in your donkey's language. Your donkey speaks the language of silence."

Comment:

This story is another example of anger damaging the aggressor more than the recipient. While language is a primary means of communication, it seems that the donkey could not have cared less as to what the owner was saying. The donkey owner's behavior was self-destructive and failed to teach the donkey anything. This may have been the first recorded instance of road rage.

Story 8: Henry Clay

Henry Clay, known as the "Great Compromiser," had a knack of settling disputes and bringing opposing parties together. After serving in the U.S. Senate for his first term, he ran for and was elected to a seat in the House of Representatives and found that he preferred to serve there. At the beginning of his first term in the House, he won election as Speaker of the House.

John Randolph was a member of the House from Virginia. His reputation was one who was very critical, rigid, and authoritarian. His behavior was often inappropriate and he would do such things as bring his dogs with him onto the floor of the House of Representatives. Before Clay arrived, the leadership had apparently been very weak. After Clay's election as Speaker, whenever Randolph would bring in his dogs, Clay would have them removed. This incensed Randolph who could be very intimidating. Randolph protested and brought the issue to a vote. The House overwhelmingly supported Clay.

Afterward, Clay and Randolph were walking on a street in Washington, D.C. approaching one another. They were moving directly on the same path. As they drew closer and closer, the tension grew. Soon they stood face to face, neither budged. Randolph said, "I never step aside for skunks!" After a moment of tense silence, Clay retorted, "I always do."

Comments:

Randolph was trying to insult Clay and create a showdown by calling him a skunk. Clay did not directly confront Randolph about being called a "skunk," though Clay did respond assertively and turned the tables. Without escalating the conflict or deferring to Randolph,

Clay was quick witted enough to allow both to save face. Clay just insisted that he employed a different tactic when it came to confronting skunks.

Story 9: Gettysburg Soldier

Beleaguered and defeated, General Robert E. Lee retreated from the battlefield at Gettysburg. As he and his officers trudged along, they came upon a Union soldier who recounted the following story.

On the last day of the battle near Cemetery Ridge, the Union soldier lay with a shattered leg. He wrote of how he hated the South and despised the Confederacy and its people. He told of how he continued to fight that day, even after he was wounded.

As Lee passed, the soldier began to taunt and deride the General. As Lee came closer, the soldier yelled louder and became more and more angry. Lee said nothing but reined his horse to near where the soldier lay. As Lee dismounted, the soldier's emotions changed. Based upon his stereotype, he thought that Lee would surely kill him and the soldier's heart filled with fear. He realized that he had allowed his anger to range out of control. As Lee approached, the soldier noticed the sad expression on the General's face, which helped diminish the soldier's fear. Lee extended his hand and firmly grasped the soldier's hand. Looking him squarely in the eyes Lee said, "My son, I wish you well. I hope that you recover soon. Your army fought bravely." The General then returned to his horse and rode off.

According to the record, the soldier said that he would never forget the expression on Lee's face as the officer wished him good will, while they remained enemies at war. He reflected upon the opposing officer whom he had taunted and of the General who had stopped to wish the wounded enemy soldier well. The soldier then said that he cried himself to sleep "upon the bloody ground."

Comments:

The image of a brave soldier of deep conviction crying himself to sleep "upon the bloody ground" is most poignant. Within the soldier, there was both the will and passion to kill the enemy as well as the tenderness and sensitivity to cry himself to sleep, after encountering the enemy from a different perspective. The combat referred to as the "Civil War" is the bloodiest and cruelest as well as the most self-destructive war in U. S. history. Some historians believe that the war could have been prevented, while others believe that if the war had not been fought the same conflicts would exist today.

There are many stories of horror concerning the war. Paradoxically, there are numerous stories of great kindness and compassion as well. The two go together. In my opinion, that is the major point of the book, *My Brother's Keeper,* by Daniel Rolph. When brother fights brother, there can be both great enmity as well as great mercy. In the book, the author tells the story of a Rebel soldier cared for by a humanitarian Union group. The soldier said, "You fight us like devils and nurse us like angels."

Conclusion: Chapter VII

Everyone experiences negative emotions such as anger, depression, and anxiety. Those who are more psychologically secure feel less threatened which helps them maintain a more flexible perspective. Beneath anger or rage there is usually fear and psychological pain or hurt. Resiliency helps prevent negative emotions from controlling our lives.

A client/patient entered psychotherapy struggling with issues of anger and depression as the result of a significant loss. In his final session, he used the analogy of driving an automobile to describe his coping with anger. He said that before therapy, "It was as though I was driving without brakes or a steering wheel. I could only use the accelerator. Now I have a steering wheel and brakes. I can speed up or slow down and can change lanes when it is necessary. I can even turn around and drive in a different direction if I need to."

Nelson Mandela spoke of living a life filled with anger and hate. He said that it was like "drinking poison while waiting for your enemy to die."

VIII: Resourceful Solutions

1. **The Lion's Whisker**
2. **The King with No Heir**
3. **Seventeen Camels**
4. **The Loan**
5. **The Pouch of Coins**
6. **The Stone Buddha**
7. **The Emperor and the Abbot**
8. **Joha's Dollar**

No significant endeavor ever goes exactly as planned. Being flexible to adapt to reality is crucial to achieving any vision or goal.

Chapter VIII presents stories that a sage or judicious mentor might offer. It presents stories of wisdom and the discovery of resourceful solutions. Exposure to alternative, creative thought engenders the same. Conventional problem solving is important but often unconventional solutions, or looking to the sea, are more important. Exposure to flexible thought and innovative solutions to problems may help open the doors of the heart and mind to recognize new possibilities.

Story 1: The Lion's Whisker

A woman married a widower who had a son. She deeply loved her husband and wanted a harmonious home life and desired to enjoy a warm relationship with her stepson. However, at every turn, the stepson rebuffed her saying, "You are not my real mother and I wish my father had never married you." He was unappreciative and scorned everything she did for him. The rejection was emotionally agonizing and eventually became unbearable for the woman. She did not want to allow her stepson's attitude to undermine her dream of establishing a pleasant home life.

One day as she was confiding her concerns to a friend, the friend told her of a man of great wisdom who lived on a deserted mountain. The friend said that she had heard of people who went to him with seemingly insurmountable problems and he would give them advice that would solve their problems. The wife asked for directions to the mountain and set out early the next morning to find the sage.

When she arrived, the wise man received her graciously and listened attentively as she presented her story. When she finished he said, "I understand your problem and will be delighted to advise you. However, yours is a particularly difficult dilemma that requires a special potion. You must pluck the whisker from a living, untamed lion in the prime of life and bring it to me for the potion." This request puzzled the woman, but she was determined to do everything she could to have a happy, harmonious home. As she walked home she thought and thought of how she might accomplish such a daunting task.

The next night she took a bowl of meat and walked out into the wilderness until she heard the roar of a lion. Hastily, she set the bowl down and ran home. Over many weeks each night she drew a little closer to the lion. After a while, she set the bowl a few feet from the lion and stood in his presence while he ate. Finally, she came to the point that she held the bowl as the lion ate and would reach out and touch the lion. Then the opportunity presented when she felt safe to pluck the whisker. She carefully secured the whisker and went home.

Exhilarated with her accomplishment, the next morning she ran to the mountain and climbed until she reached the home of the sage. He was sitting warming by a fire. He accepted the whisker from the woman, examined it carefully, and acknowledged that it met the demands. Suddenly, to her horror, he tossed the whisker into the fire. The woman was exasperated. She asked, "Do you realize how much time, patience, and effort I invested into acquiring that whisker? I can't believe that you just took a brief look and discarded it." The wise man replied, "You are correct. It did take great patience and bravery to accomplish such a great task. But I also realize that anyone who has the courage, determination, and ingenuity to gain the trust of a ferocious beast has what it takes to gain the trust of an angry boy."

Comments:

The story almost has a cruel twist to it. However, the sage did a great favor by helping the woman discover that she could solve a problem that she did not realize that she could solve. I doubt that the sage would have been of much help if he had said, "You are a bright person. I'm sure you can find a way to solve this problem. Just think about it." She would probably have interpreted the advice as being of little value. She even may have been insulted. She might have said, "If I knew how to solve the problem, I sure as heck wouldn't have taken the time and effort to come to see you." She needed the experience of discovering what she could do.

She was clever. She was a behavioral psychologist even before there was such. She employed what became termed as "successive approximation" and what B. F. Skinner called operant conditioning to accomplish her goal. She gradually came closer and closer, reinforcing the lion until she could touch him. Accomplishing what she did gave her a new perspective and confidence.

Another significant feature of this story is the woman's motivation and persistence. She was tenacious. Stories of success emphasize that persistence is as important, if not more important, than anything else. How many times has the quote of Thomas Edison been cited: "Genius is one percent inspiration and ninety-nine percent perspiration"? This woman had a wealth of both. This is another example of someone discovering that the solution comes from within though she was looking outwardly for help. She discovered that she knew more than she thought she did.

Have you ever climbed a mountain that you initially thought was impossible to climb? Have you ever faced a loss that you thought you could not survive? At one time it seemed inconceivable, yet you not only survived but once again came to live and thrive. As we reflect on our lives, I would imagine that everyone could cite an example. Each could tell such a story or two or three. In the words of Napoleon Hill,

"Effort fully releases its reward after a person refuses to quit."

Story 2: The King with No Heir

Known for his honesty and character, a wise king ruled a great kingdom. The subjects were content, considered the king just, and perceived him as being concerned about the people's interests. The king possessed great wealth and he and the queen were happy except for one concern. They had no children, thus no heir to the kingdom. The king's advisors observed that as he grew older the king became preoccupied with worry about the future of the kingdom. The advisors became concerned for the king as well as anxious about their futures.

After much thought, the king decided upon a plan to solve the problem. He sent out messengers throughout the regions of the kingdom extending an invitation for all subjects to come to the palace for an important meeting. The king announced that since he had no heirs to the kingdom that he would select one from among the people. He then told them of the manner in which he would make the decision.

He presented each of his subjects with a flowerpot that contained a planted seed. He told them to grow only their seed, the one planted in their pot, and to water and nourish it as they saw fit. He declared that he would judge the contest based upon who produced the best results from the seed given to the person. The winner would become heir to the kingdom. He announced that they were to return with their plants on a designated date and that all the plants would be displayed on the palace grounds. Furthermore, the king stated that there would be a festival and that he would announce the heir to the kingdom on the final day of celebration. The king reasoned that whoever was diligent in managing small matters would be diligent in large matters such as ruling the kingdom.

The people of the kingdom were excited. As they returned to their respective villages, they discussed their skills and strategies for growing plants. After a few months, the people returned to the capitol palace with their plants. Some of the subjects did not return with their flowerpots explaining that they did not have a "green thumb" or that they had no interest in being an heir. Many people did bring plants and were pleased to display them at the palace.

The ministers and advisors were astonished at the beauty of the plants. Most plants were in bloom and the colors and fragrances were astounding. The people spent many hours strolling the grounds and viewing the plants. The ministers thought that it would be impossible to choose one from among so many lovely plants. Near the end of the exhibit, a subject brought in a pot for display that contained a cocklebur plant, a weed. The plant was unattractive with its prickly burs and detracted from the display. The crowd mocked and ridiculed the subject.

On the day of the announcement, the king accompanied by his entourage reviewed the plants. The king admired the beauty of the plants and was impressed at the talent of his subjects. The king consulted with his advisors who were dumbfounded and saw no way that the king could make a definite decision on which plant to choose.

As the king addressed the people of his kingdom, he complimented them for their ability to produce large, beautiful plants. He expressed appreciation for the time and effort that they had spent. The king called attention to the cocklebur pot and asked his advisors to bring it to him. They set the pot before the king. Then, the king asked for the owner of the pot containing the burry weed to raise his hand. He was isolated at the back of the crowd. The people laughed and jeered.

Slowly, the man came forward with his head and shoulders erect without knowing what to expect wondering if he would be a spectacle of ridicule. The subject apologized for the looks of his plant but explained that he had carefully watered and fertilized it and saw to it that it had plenty of sun.

The king then placed his hand on the young man's shoulder and said to the gathering, "Please meet the heir to the kingdom." The crowd grew deathly silent. After a latent pause, the king announced that all of the seeds that he had given out were weeds. Many had found other seeds to plant in their pots. Some thought that their seed had died or that the wind had blown the seed of a weed into their pots. Some were just conniving. Others became discouraged and gave up when they found only a weed growing in their pot. They felt embarrassed and anticipated derision.

The king said, "I want my heir to be a person of integrity, one who can withstand public disapproval and one who will do his very best with the resources available." Again, there was silence. As the people thought, they agreed. The consensus was that the king had made a wise decision.

Comments:

Character matters. In this case, even those who had changed seeds agreed. The king wanted a person of integrity to rule the throne. He wanted someone uncontrolled by public opinion or disapproval, qualities which are crucial to character.

The people assumed that the winner would be the person with the most beautiful plant. After all, is not that what most plant contests are about? The king did not say that the person who produced the largest or most beautiful plant would win. The one who did one's best with the seed given would become the heir. Is not that what resiliency is about— doing the best one can with what one has?

In addition, a comment upon the issue of heirs is in order. Such stories as this can arouse sensitive emotions in those who want children and cannot have them as well as those who have lost children or heirs. My heart goes out to those who have known such experiences. Often those who have no children are the most caring and nurturing.

Note: Cockleburs (Xanthium strumarium) are small football shaped prickly burs, which contain a seed. They are roughly the size of a pinto bean and stick to clothing and fur similar to Velcro. The number of varieties is debatable; however, they have spread all over the world. The seeds are poisonous and are a potential danger to livestock. The flowering plants have been used to produce yellow dye and for medicinal purposes in China. Children play with cockleburs and stick them together to create models and throw them at one another since they adhere so readily to cloth.

Story 3: Seventeen Camels

A father died and specified in his will that his estate of seventeen camels was to be divided among his three sons. The will clearly stated that one-half be given to the eldest son, one-third to the second son, and one-ninth to the youngest son. No camel could be slaughtered or sold. Each of the sons respected the father's will. The problem was that seventeen was not evenly divisible equally into the designated proportions. Half of seventeen would be eight and one-half.

Standing around the corral one morning, the sons began an argument that continued for weeks. The eldest son stated that they should round off eight and one-half to nine and divide the rest between the younger brothers. The youngest brother retorted, "If anyone should be given an extra camel, it should be me since I am receiving the least number." The brothers argued, fumed and fought but made no progress. Word was spreading about the sons' bickering.

Hearing of the quarreling, a wise uncle visited to see if he could offer assistance. He said, "I can see your problem. There is no way to divide seventeen into the proportions set by your father in his will." He thought for a while then said, "I believe I may have a solution if you are willing to trust me. But you must be willing to accept my solution and stop your bickering." The sons agreed and said that next to their father, the uncle was the man that they respected and trusted most.

The uncle then led his camel into the corral with the seventeen. He said to the eldest, "Now there are eighteen camels; take your half which is nine." The oldest son separated his nine from the rest. The uncle said to the second son, "There are nine left. Take your portion of one-third which is six." He did. Then to the youngest son the uncle said, "Take your portion of one-ninth which is two." He separated his two, which left one, the uncle's camel.

He then said to his nephews, "Your father was not a foolish man. He knew the number of camels that he owned. Why do you suppose that he left such a problematic will?" No longer were the brothers quarreling.

Together, they began to think of possibilities. After a while, one son asked, "Uncle, why do you think he left such a will?" The uncle stated, "I will not offer an opinion. This is not the last time that the three of you will quarrel. You must learn to find solutions together and work in harmony rather than reacting with acrimony. Pondering the question together is a good place for you to begin." The uncle then mounted his camel and started home. Behind, the three sons sat and discussed possibilities until late into the night.

Comments:

Times and cultures change. In some cultures, especially in ancient times, giving the oldest son all or most of the inheritance was considered appropriate. Today, most would consider the father's distribution unfair. Other things do not change. Inheritance issues can create great strife and divide families. Why did the father leave such a will? Sometimes ancestors try to provoke enmity and hostility through their bequests, but that explanation would not apply in this case.

The young men were fortunate to have an uncle with wisdom who cared and approached them. It would have shown greater maturity if they had called upon the uncle instead. Though the uncle's solution was clever and satisfied the sons, the older son still gained an extra "half camel." One might question how adept the younger two brothers were at math. The uncle did nudge them toward more independence and maturity by having them discuss the reason for the oddly written will, while declining to think for them.

Story 4: The Loan

One night a friend knocked on Joha's door. He pleaded for a loan and assured Joha that he would repay it in two weeks. Joha thought for a while and winced to see his friend in such a state of distress. Against his better judgment, Joha granted his friend the loan. Joha was surprised when his friend arrived in exactly a fortnight and repaid the loan. A few months passed and Joha again heard a knock at his door. As Joha opened the door, he saw his friend again requesting another loan. Joha refused and said, "Absolutely not. The last time I loaned you money, I did not expect you to repay it. You surprised me and did. I refuse to give you the opportunity to fool me again."

Comments:

Joha was wise to be cautious when it came to lending money. My sister offers an interesting strategy for dealing with people who want to borrow money. When people ask, she suggests saying, "Nothing personal, but I am such a poor judge of character that I can't trust my own judgment." When they try to reassure her about their honesty, she says, "I'm not questioning your integrity. It is just that I can't trust my judgment."

My philosophy can be expressed: Do not lend books or unsecured money to anyone you know or do not know. Offer a gift if the person is truly in need. Friendships become estranged and people avoid you when they owe you money. In addition, one of the oldest tricks of psychopaths and con artists is to borrow money and pay it back promptly for a time or two and then borrow more and disappear. Perhaps Joha knew of the age-old practice.

There is a Mark Twain story of a visitor coming by Twain's residence in Hartford. Twain cautioned the visitor not to stumble over a large stack of books on the floor. Twain apologized for the untidiness and added, "It is so much more difficult to borrow bookshelves than books."

Story 5: The Pouch

A peasant was walking down a crowded street. People were bumping him on the right and left. Standing by their carts, merchants were shouting to attract attention to sell their goods. As the peasant looked down, he noticed a leather pouch lying in the street and picked it up. He nudged his way to an alley and opened the pouch. To his surprise, it contained gold coins. He counted them and there were one hundred. Soon he heard the cry of a solicitor yelling "REWARD! REWARD! to anyone who has found a leather pouch. REWARD! REWARD! to anyone who has found a leather pouch."

Being an honest man, the poor peasant raised the pouch of coins and waved to the finely dressed solicitor. The solicitor approached and aggressively grabbed for the bag. The peasant pulled back and said, "Not so fast. Let's discuss the reward." The solicitor asked, "What is in the pouch?" The peasant said, "Gold coins." "How many," inquired the counselor? "One hundred," was the reply. "You thief," screamed the solicitor. "Why, an hour ago there were two hundred coins in the pouch. I'll give you no reward. You already have more than a fair reward." The solicitor berated the poor peasant until he would listen no longer. The peasant said that the only way he knew to solve the case was to present it before a judge. "Very well," said the greedy solicitor.

They entered the court and awaited their turn. Then each explained his case. The judge patiently listened. When it came time for the verdict, the judge paused in thought. He then turned to the peasant and said, "The pouch that you found had one hundred coins. Is that correct?" "Yes," replied the peasant. Then, turning to the solicitor the judge asked, "And the pouch you lost contained two hundred coins." The solicitor said, "Yes." The judge turned to the peasant and issued his verdict: "Obviously, the pouch that you found is not his. You may keep the pouch and I would suggest that your accuser return to the street immediately to search for the pouch that he lost."

Comments:

The solicitor outwitted himself. His greed cost him all of his coins. In this instance, honesty prevailed.

Story 6: The Stone Buddha

A struggling merchant traveled a great distance to purchase rolls of cotton that he could sell in his store. He considered himself fortunate that he could borrow money to purchase his goods. He could not afford a donkey; therefore, the merchant pulled a small cart. As he returned from his long journey, he pulled the cart loaded with rolls of cotton cloth. One day in the hot midday sun, he approached a village.

Exhausted from his efforts, he parked his cart at the side of the road before entering the village. There was a small shaded park at the entrance of the town with a stone statue of the Buddha. The man pulled his cart near the statue and lay on the ground napping for an hour.

When he awoke, to his dismay all of his prized rolls of cotton were missing. Panicked he ran through the street shouting, "I was robbed! I was robbed! Where is the constable?" Upon hearing the story the chief constable scratched his head and said, "This is most unusual. We rarely experience any crime in our village. We must consult the judge." The merchant told the judge his story of napping near the statue of the Buddha and his rolls of cotton cloth disappearing.

The judge declared, "This is most outrageous. I hereby demand the stone Buddha arrested and brought before the court." The judge ordered the constable to gather a group of citizens and bring the stone Buddha into the courtroom. The decision created quite a murmur among the town folk as they crowded into the courtroom.

After the group situated the statue, the judge asked, "How do you plead?" The people of the town erupted in laughter. "Order, order!" exclaimed the judge. "One more outburst and I will arrest all of you for contempt of court." The judge proceeded with his interrogation of the stone Buddha but there was no response. Soon the people of the town could resist no longer. They burst out again in laughter at such a ridiculous sight. The judge announced that everyone in the entire town was under arrest for contempt of court and would be sentenced to a term in jail.

As the townspeople beseeched for relief, the judge said, "Perhaps I was a bit rash. I will give you one option. Citizens who bring in a roll of cotton cloth by midday tomorrow will have their charge dropped. But I warn you, anyone who does not will receive an extensive term of confinement." The people mumbled and muttered but did as the judge had ordered and began to bring rolls of cloth into the courtroom.

After a while, the merchant recognized one of the rolls as coming from his inventory. He told the judge, who in turn, had the constable arrest the person with the merchant's roll and had the thief retrieve the remaining rolls. The merchant gathered his goods, thanked everyone, and returned to his travel. The judge then informed the people of the village that they could take back their rolls of cloth.

Comments:

What may seem foolish, cruel, or ridiculous at one level may have a deeper strategy or purpose at another and prove clever. The judge knew what he was doing. His thought reflected flexibility. He used an unorthodox strategy, predating Detective Columbo, to solve a crime.

Story 7: The Emperor and the Abbot

An emperor was inclined to travel about his kingdom to observe the people. Once, he came upon a monastery. Over the gate, he found the following words carved in stone: "Here one lives without a care." The sentiment struck an emotional chord with the emperor who asked, "How is this possible? How can anyone live without a care? I have problems and decisions to deal with each day that produce much worry."

The emperor sent for the abbot of the monastery to come visit him at the inn nearby where he and his entourage lodged. The abbot was a cheerful man with a round face but he could not help but feel anxious about what the emperor might want. The abbot went to the inn, and as he entered, addressed the emperor with the appropriate protocol. The emperor remarked that he had seen the engraving over the gate to the monastery:

"Here one lives without a care." The emperor asked, "How can this be?"

The abbot said that we pray and do our work. When we are sleepy we sleep, when we are thirsty, we drink, and when we are hungry we eat. We have no reason to worry.

The emperor listened and thought for a moment then said, "I am going to present three questions to you. You are to return tomorrow at noon with the answers. If you fail to answer these questions to my satisfaction, I assure you that you will have something about which to worry. There will be dire consequences.

The emperor presented the questions:

1. "How deep is the sea?"
2. "How many cows' tails would it take to reach the moon?"
3. "What am I thinking?"

The emperor asked, "Do you understand?" The abbot repeated each of the questions:

1. "How deep is the sea?"
2. "How many cows' tails would it take to reach the moon?"
3. "What am I thinking?"

The emperor said, "I will expect you back tomorrow at noon with the answers."

The abbot left and shuffled along back to the monastery. His posture was slumped, his eyes downcast, and for the first time he realized what it meant to worry. When he reached the monastery, he paced up and down the hall ruminating about what would become of the monastery. He thought, "I will never be able to answer such complicated questions." He walked out to the garden where he had enjoyed so many pleasant moments absorbing the radiant colors and fragrance of the flowers; however, this time they brought him no enjoyment.

Absorbed in thought, he walked across the meadow until he eventually came to a pasture where the shepherd tended the monasteries' flock. The shepherd had a similar build as the abbot. As the shepherd greeted the abbot, he noticed that something was wrong. The shepherd said, "In all the years I have known you, I have never seen you dejected. What is the matter?" At first, the abbot avoided answering but the shepherd insisted. The abbot told the shepherd that he had met with the emperor who said that the abbot must answer three questions by tomorrow at noon or there would be severe repercussions.

The shepherd asked, "What are the questions?" The abbot repeated them:

1. "How deep is the sea?"
2. "How many cows' tails would it take to reach the moon?"
3. "What am I thinking?"

The shepherd said, "Do not worry about it. I can take care of the problem." The abbot said, "What do you mean? I cannot put you in such a compromising position. Who knows what might happen to both of us? We are dealing with the emperor!" However, the shepherd confidently insisted and finally convinced the abbot. The shepherd added, "There is one provision. I must stop by the monastery and borrow your robe in the morning when I go to visit the emperor." Reluctantly, the abbot agreed to the shepherd's plan.

Adorned in the abbot's robe and hood, the shepherd went to the inn to meet with the emperor at the appointed time. The emperor received him and asked, "Do you have the answers to my questions?" The shepherd responded affirmatively. The emperor asked, "What is the depth of the sea?" The shepherd replied, "A stone's throw." The emperor said, "Very well, I will accept that." Next, "How many cows' tails would it take to reach the moon?" "Sire, it will take only one, if it were long enough."

The emperor said, "Now for the most difficult question: What am I thinking?" The shepherd said, "You are thinking that I am the abbot. However, I am merely a shepherd."

After a moment of silence, the emperor erupted in laughter. He laughed and laughed. Soon the members of the court joined in chorus. When the emperor composed himself he said, "Return to the monastery and tell the abbot and the monks that because of you, they may now live without a care."

Comments:

The question was presented: How can one live without a care, without stress? Inquiring minds want to know. The emperor did not know peace. He knew that he did not know peace. He had important decisions to make and problems to solve. It puzzled and annoyed him that others might live carefree, stress-free lives.

Did the abbot truly know what it was to live without a care? The emperor presented a trial, a test. The abbot who represents an authority, who not only knows peace but also teaches others to live by faith and find peace, discovered that he was not the authority that he thought he was. The abbot came to know anxiety. Perhaps his circumscribed life of solitude and limited contact with the world only offered a pseudo-peace, superficial peace. The abbot discovered that questions of great magnitude baffled him.

The lowly shepherd who lived outside the monastery, in nature, and who tended sheep, provided the answers. He is the one who really knew what it meant to live without a care. His mind was not congested with concrete, limiting thoughts, and assumptions. The humble shepherd saved the day and amused the emperor. The emperor erupted in hearty laughter, thus experiencing the moment and enjoying a carefree minute of peace.

The educated abbot did not possess the plasticity of thought to answer the questions. The shepherd did.

Story 8: Joha's Dollar

A wealthy sultan had five sons. He believed that traveling and visiting diverse cultures was the best way to educate his sons. Before they settled down to assume their administrative roles, he urged them to see as much of the world as possible. While returning home from visiting Australia, the brothers passed through Joha's village.

One of their father's friends resided in the village. When the brothers met their father's friend, the host insisted that they accept his hospitality and stay with him for as long as they wished before proceeding on their journey. The brothers were weary from travel and accepted the invitation. They decided to stay in the village for two weeks. Each day the brothers visited the coffee shop that Joha frequented. Upon entering the coffee shop, Joha noticed a group of strangers sitting at a table sipping coffee as they talked and laughed. One of the strangers was holding an odd-looking, elbow shaped object made of wood. Joha was so curious that he could not resist asking the man what he was holding. The stranger said, "It is called a boomerang. We have recently returned from Australia where we found it."

Joha and the brothers exchanged introductions and the brothers invited Joha to join them. Joha asked, "Is it true that when it is summer here that it is winter in Australia?" The visitors replied in the affirmative. Joha explained that he had never had the opportunity to travel much and had never gone far from his village. Joha began to ask question after question about places that the sons had traveled.

One of the brothers was a trickster and surmised that Joha was rather dim-witted and naive. He had a sack of coins that he had brought back from Australia. He reached in his sack and took out two Australian coins. One was a one-dollar coin and the other was a two-dollar coin. In Australia, the one-dollar coin is larger than the two-dollar coin. The trickster told Joha that one of the coins was worth twice as much as the other and that Joha could have whichever he chose. Joha thought for a moment then picked up the larger, one-dollar coin. The brothers giggled and snickered as Joha took his coin and announced that it was time for him to go home to spend the evening with his wife.

The next day when Joha visited the coffee shop, he found the brothers sitting at the same table. He asked to join them and they received him. All of the brothers perceived Joha to be affable but gullible. Especially, the trickster enjoyed exploiting Joha's naivety. For example, the trickster relished telling Joha of unicorns.

As Joha prepared to leave, again, the trickster presented the same choice of coins and asked, "Which coin would you choose?" For a second time, Joha took the one-dollar coin. Again, the men laughed as Joha left.

After a few days, four of the brothers felt sympathy for Joha and repeatedly asked, "Why do you take the same coin each time. Why don't you choose the other one sometime?" Joha said, "I don't know, I guess I just prefer larger coins." The same event took place every day for two weeks until the brothers announced that they would be leaving the next day. Word spread around the village of Joha's apparent folly and as the townspeople caught on regarding the value of the coins, they began to jeer and giggle as Joha left each day.

On the day before the brothers left, Joha met them at the coffee shop for the last visit. Joha thanked them for sharing so much information about their world adventures. As the time came for the conversation to end, the townspeople in the coffee shop were eager to see if Joha would have the opportunity to choose between the coins. The trickster reached for the two coins, placed them on the table, and told Joha that he could choose the one he wanted. Joha immediately picked up the smaller two-dollar coin. The trickster was astounded and it seemed that collectively the crowd's mouth dropped open.

One of the more empathetic brothers explained, "It may not seem logical but the smaller coin is a two-dollar coin. It is worth twice as much as the larger one-dollar coin. Why did you choose the one-dollar coin each time until today? You could have had twice the amount of money."

Joha replied, "Let me explain, I have a small collection of coins and have a little knowledge about coin collecting and numismatics. My reasoning was as follows: how many times do you think that he, the trickster, would have offered me the choice of the two coins if I had selected the two-dollar coin the first time? You are mistaken when you say that I would have twice the amount of money. I have many times more money now than I would have if I had chosen the two-dollar coin the first day."

The empathetic brother said to Joha, "It turns out that the joke was on us. By the way, in case you haven't already surmised, there is no such animal as a unicorn."

Comments:

The motif of this story comes from Edward de Bono who told a story of a boy named Johnny. Dr. de Bono is a medical doctor from Malta who was educated in Great Britain; however, he has spent his life investigating thinking, creativity and problem solving. As far as I know, American psychology has paid little attention to his work and some have demeaned his books by calling them "pop psychology." However, he consults with organizations internationally and seems well respected by the corporate world.

He is famous for creating the term "lateral thinking." One of his major contributions has been the differentiation between what he calls "rock logic" and "water logic." He says that Western thinking has largely followed rock logic and built upon the reasoning of Aristotle, Plato, and Socrates. Rock logic is fixed.

Whether in a bucket, on a table, or held in one's hand, a rock maintains its shape and content. Rock logic deals with "is." In the previous story, rock logic dealt with what "is" the value of the coins. The title of one of de Bono's books, *I'm Right and You are Wrong,* illustrates rock logic. Rock logic is adversarial; you are innocent or guilty, right or wrong.

On the other hand, water logic is resilient; water logic is fluid. When you pour water into a container, it conforms to the container's shape. Water will conform to the shape of a glass, jar or vase. Water may exist in solid, liquid, or gas form. According to de Bono, water logic deals with perception and "to."

In the previous story, Joha was concerned with what his decision about the coin would lead "to." The trickster used rock logic, while Joha used water logic. If Joha kept choosing the one-dollar coin, the trickster would continue to demonstrate, or perceive Joha's "lack of reasoning," in terms of rock logic, and continue offering Joha opportunities to appear "foolish" though from Joha's perspective he was accumulating more and more money.

Another point from the story is that the sons were most fortunate to have a father who was seriously interested in their overall educations and wise enough to appreciate the importance of travel as education. As importantly, the brothers were fortunate that the father was wealthy enough to provide the sons with the opportunity to travel.

On the other hand, it is most unfortunate when those blessed with privilege and advantages do not appreciate their good fortune, and the responsibilities associated therewith. It is even worse when those born into privilege use their benefits to take advantage of and even exploit those whom they perceive to be vulnerable and naïve.

Joha sought knowledge and learned of far away cultures. The trickster mistakenly believed that he had nothing to learn from Joha. Though not seeking knowledge, the trickster learned a lesson from Joha. The desire to discover, to learn, is a key attribute in developing resilience.

Conclusion: Chapter VIII

Advice is plentiful. Good advice is often expensive but the same applies to bad counsel. Decisions as to whom to listen and whom to ignore are some of the most important choices in life. My observation is that resourceful, successful people make much better choices as to who to listen to for advice and who to ignore for advice. It is very important to know who to listen to when gathering important information to make decisions.

In addressing creativity some make the distinction between the big "C' and the little "c." The *C* refers to major creative discoveries such as Einstein's Theory of Relativity. The *c* refers to problem solving activities. Both involve bringing together two planes of thoughts that are not ordinarily associated.

Once, I had the good fortune of hearing the famous developmental psychologist, Jean Piaget, speak at Johns Hopkins University. He recommended four steps to creatively solving problems. 1. Go as far as you can with your own thinking. Do not read or listen to what others have to say. 2. When you can go no further, read and listen to what others have to say in your discipline. 3. Then, read other disciplines. 4. Put yourself in the position of someone skeptical of your solution and think of what a critic might say.

Resolving life problems and discovering creative solutions are vital to living well.

IX: Conclusion

W. Faulkner

Chapter IX presents a statement of faith in humankind's ability to not only survive but thrive. It comes from William Faulkner's speech in accepting the Noble Prize in Literature.

Story: William Faulkner

William Faulkner expressed faith in the human spirit in his speech accepting the Nobel Prize in Literature in Paris in 1950. He said, "I believe that man will not merely endure: he will prevail." Faulkner went on to say that it is the writer's "duty" and "privilege" to call readers' attention to the qualities of the human spirit— such as courage, compassion, hope, and sacrifice— that have served in the past and can continue to promote survival and triumph.

Comments:

Distinguished literature addresses the qualities of which Faulkner spoke. It can promote resilience and teach important life lessons as well as expose vulnerabilities to human foibles. Reading of courage, compassion, hope and sacrifice in others can encourage our developing such qualities that help us endure and thrive. Though not necessarily a great role model, Faulkner did possess strengths and expressed deep belief that humankind would survive and thrive.

Conclusion: Chapters I—IX

Stories that guide us to psychological resiliency take into account discovering and prioritizing that which is of value, which includes our strengths, as well as building relationships. In addition, accepting what we cannot change in life, changing what we can, while having the wisdom to discern the difference is a vital part of life's journey. Recognizing and dealing effectively with folly and negative emotions are aspects to building resiliency. Having the flexibility of perception to view obstacles from diverse viewpoints is of significant value in accessing life solutions.

Our nature and environments significantly determine our lives; however, we have choices as well. One choice is to exercise and nourish our strengths rather than to hopelessly ruminate upon our inadequacies.

Another choice involves where we place our focus temporally. Should we focus primarily upon the past, the present or the future? Often, psychotherapists associate psychopathology with obsessing upon the past or future while failing to live in or accept the present. Attending to the past, present, and future are each important in guiding us through life. It is obsessing upon one, at the expense of the others, that is maladaptive. Psychological resilience requires learning from the past and looking toward the future while living in the present.

Stories from the past teach us lessons in the present and guide us toward the future. Not only individuals, but also the collective human family should learn from the past, look toward the future, and accept and live in the present.

Joy and sorrow are mingled into the fabric of life. Weddings and births are celebrated each day just as infirmities and funerals are mourned. Joseph Campbell said, "We are here to participate joyfully in the sorrows of the world." Campbell believed deeply that stories, in various forms, play an invaluable role in invigorating the strength to maintain balance and perspective as we participate in the journey through the world of joy and sorrow.

Final Words

People do not live to be two or three thousand years old, but their stories do. Stories of wisdom that teach important lessons of life bless the recipient as well as the storyteller. Stories passed down from generation to generation connect us with all humankind and may bring us as close to immortality as we can experience in this life.

We shall end where we began. In the beginning, before there were psychologists, consultants, and experts, there were stories. After there are psychologists, consultants, and experts, there will still be stories.

The End

(Addendums follow)

Addendums

Addendum I:

Introduction

Although psychology as a discipline in the United States has focused primarily upon pathology for the past six decades, an expanding interest in qualities that help one move beyond just coping has recently emerged. "Psychological resilience" is one of many psychological terms that overlap in meaning and have much in common. Sometimes various terms are applied almost synonymously. Other terms include: positive psychology, flourishing, thriving, emotional intelligence, and learned optimism. In addition, happiness, search for meaning, and self-actualization are used. The study of the psychological and physical benefits of humor fits within the general umbrella as well.

The factor that all of these terms have in common is that they focus upon psychological well being, developing strengths, and constructive aspects of psychological potential rather than upon mental illness and disorders. The focus is upon building strengths and abilities rather than expelling debilities. Another conviction that they hold in common is that the absence of mental illness does not mean that one enjoys optimum mental health or well-being.

Today, the term "positive psychology" is more popular than the other terms. However, I prefer "resilience and thriving." While I believe that those who use the term "positive psychology" have no intention of implying that traditional approaches to treating disorders are negative, it seems reasonable to me that readers may be tempted to infer that "non-positive" approaches are negative. After all, the opposite of positive is negative. Furthermore, terms such as positive psychology, positive thinking, and optimism have great variations in meaning and are easily confused.

Psychological resilience is "the process of adapting well in the face of adversity, trauma, tragedy, threats, or even significant sources of stress...." (American Psychological Association)

As used in this publication, resilience goes beyond just coping, adapting, and adjusting and incorporates both surviving and thriving. One may even find joy and meaning in life while enduring hardships.

The psychologically resilient face adversity; however, they do not allow their hardships to define them. While facing significant life stressors results in emotional pain and discomfort, the more resilient tend to grow from having experienced adversity rather than languishing as a result.

Dr. Paul Pearsall often compared the physical immune system to what he called the "psychological immune system." Just as with the body's immune system, not everyone exposed to a virus or bacteria will contract a disease. In fact, most people who encounter disease-producing entities do not develop the disease. Their immune systems are strong enough to resist. The psychological immune system is analogous to the physical immune system in that not every stressor results in a psychological disorder. The stronger the psychological immune system, the more psychologically resilient one is. Of course, individuals' psychological immune systems vary not only in strength but in areas of vulnerability. Some are more susceptible to certain stressors and symptoms than others. For example, individuals vary regarding their vulnerability to anxiety, depression, and anger.

Addendum II:

More About Psychological Resilience

1. **Beethoven**
2. **Liz Murray**

As a child, I remember that on hot summer nights, my parents would take my sister and me to revival services at churches for many miles and in all directions. Two familiar denominations in our region held very similar doctrines except for a few beliefs. In revival services, they focused attention upon their differences.

One denomination emphasized grace and believed in what was commonly termed, "justification by faith alone" or sometimes referred to as "once saved always saved." A very oversimplified explanation of the doctrine is that once you have expressed faith in Jesus Christ nothing could interfere with your salvation. The other denomination emphasized works. An oversimplification of their doctrine was that you are saved by your "good works." Though few psychologists, whom I have encountered, consider themselves religious many do hold strongly to a version of the first doctrine noted. Many believe that "once traumatized, always traumatized or once victimized always victimized."

A secret, which I hope is less closely guarded now, is that most people successfully survive and adequately cope with stress, crises, and trauma, as well as exposure to dysfunctional families, and do so regularly without professional help.

In some cases professional mental health treatment may be called for over a limited period. The importance, need, and benefit of professional mental health assistance should not be discounted or minimized. However, excessive emphasis by professionals or society upon traumatic events or victimization and the permanence of symptoms can result in a self-fulfilling prophecy.

In addition, to say that most survivors cope without professional help or a limited period of professional help does not mean that they do not experience mental anguish. Nor does it mean that they do not receive emotional and social support. They may find a strong support system in family, friends, or church. They may receive encouragement and guidance from a parent, grandparent, mentor, or colleague.

Reportedly, Albert Bandura is the most cited, referenced, psychologist in the world. In a speech to the Canadian Psychological Association, he stated that psychology "is infected with a virulent negativity virus" which leads to "grossly over predicting psychopathology."

He added that according to psychological theories one would expect that children who grow up in environments of poverty and abuse would develop into adults who are psychologically maladjusted and destined for a life of crime, pathology, and addiction. Dr. Bandura points out that, to the contrary, most children who grow up in "psycho-social risky environments" become responsible adults who are able to relate to others and contribute to society. They may stumble and struggle but in time find their way.

An interesting study was conducted by Elizabeth Newton; it involved tapping the tunes of songs. Tappers were given a list of simple, well-known songs and asked to use their fingers to tap the song for a listener. Before they tapped, Dr. Newton asked the tappers to predict what percentage of people would recognize the song. The tappers predicted that fifty percent of the listeners would recognize the song. One-hundred-twenty songs were tapped. How many did the listeners identify? Three! That is two and one-half percent or one in forty.

Why were the tappers such poor predictors? The reason was that the tappers could not tap the tune without hearing it themselves. They "played the songs mentally." Listeners did not have the advantage of "hearing the song in their heads." Once you have knowledge, it is very difficult to place yourself in the position of someone who does not. Research reveals that people who have learned a task tend to predict that others can learn the task much faster than they actually can. Some refer to the phenomenon as the "curse of knowledge" or being "overly optimistic." Conversely, could it be that knowledge of psychological symptoms, diagnoses, and theories influence psychologists to be "overly pessimistic" or "infected with the virulent negative virus"?

Following are two stories that present examples of people who overcame great obstacles and demonstrated psychological resiliency

Story 1: Beethoven

An important book on thriving amidst adversity is *The Beethoven Factor* by Paul Pearsall. Beethoven began having serious hearing problems in early adulthood. By age twenty-six, he suffered from severe tinnitus, ringing in his ears, which interfered with his enjoying music and conversation. His hearing loss became worse until he eventually became deaf. Living in poverty, at age thirty-one, he became so hopeless, despondent, and depressed that he was suicidal. He continued to have depressive episodes off and on throughout his life, yet he continued to compose.

As his hearing deteriorated, he attached a rod to a soundboard on a piano. He would bite the rod and the vibrations of the music would resonate through his jaw. On one occasion, he was leading the orchestra with his eyes closed. The orchestra stopped playing when the crowd arose to give Beethoven a roaring standing ovation. Beethoven continued to direct the orchestra. Someone from the choir approached Beethoven and gently turned him around so that he could see the audience. Tears of joy filled his eyes as he observed the scene. Ironically, the composition that he was performing was "Ode to Joy," which is in his Ninth Symphony. The event occurred over twenty years after he had been suicidal.

Beethoven struggled and had his flaws. He could not bring himself to tell strangers of his hearing loss or ask them to speak louder or repeat themselves. He distained social rank while pretending to be of noble descent until he accidentally disclosed his deceit.

He did keep "conversation books" in which he wrote notes to friends and often they responded in writing. Later in life, he wrote of being as happy as possible and of seizing "fate by the throat." Beethoven had a close group of supportive friends who saw him as having a strong personality. Though he could not hear, he would play notes and humorously comment to friends as to how beautiful "they sounded."

In addition to the composer dealing with deafness, his treatment or "mistreatment" by his physician did not help. The physician prescribed large doses of lead that resulted in lead poisoning and gastrointestinal pain and likely shortened his life.

Comments:

For a music composer, what could be more threatening than the loss of hearing? It usually takes time to accept and adapt to loss. It took Beethoven time. His depression did not end after one episode. He continued to struggle and learned to adapt. Combining talent with persistence, he became one of the greatest composers in history.

Beethoven was unusual in a way. I have seen many people over the years who were depressed at the permanent loss of sensory and other physical abilities. Most have to give up what gave them meaning, purpose, and pleasure in life and discover an alternative avenue. For most, that is an extremely challenging adjustment. First, they have to accept the loss, which is difficult; however, usually what is most threatening and alarming is the journey to find meaning and purpose in other ways. Beethoven found avenues to continue composing despite being deaf.

"The Beethoven Factor" serves as a powerful example of resilience and thriving. Furthermore, it underscores that acquiring these qualities does not mean the elimination of struggle and challenge.

Not all resilient people are identical. All are unique but have many qualities in common and they tend to appreciate their unique qualities as well as the unique qualities of others. Some develop certain qualities more than others do. A continuum rather than a dichotomy is a better perspective to view psychological resilience. It is not something that you either have or do not have but rather it exists in degrees. Further, the literature suggests that it is never too late to develop resilience. One may start at age three or ninety-three; however the younger the better.

Flow is a term often associated with resilience, thriving, and positive psychology. From the description of Beethoven, while conducting the *Ode to Joy* in his Ninth Symphony, he may well have been in a state of flow.

Though the experience has existed for ages, the term *flow* was proposed, studied and researched by Dr. Mihaly Csikszentimihalyi. He popularized and discussed the term in his books, *Flow: The Psychology of Optimal Experience* and in *Creativity: Flow and the Psychology of Discovery and Invention.*

Those experiencing flow become immersed, focused, and totally engaged, in what they are doing. One loses sense of time and self-consciousness. “Being in the zone,” “in the groove” or “on a roll” are colloquial terms that are similar and expressions with which most can identify. Action is effortless and experienced as intrinsically rewarding. It occurs when people use their strengths and talents and are working on a task that is challenging to them but attainable. Flow may occur while creating a work of art, performing a sport, conducting research, or creating an invention.

Beethoven, Helen Keller, and Abraham Lincoln are examples of resilient people who were famous. Another is Nelson Mandela who demonstrated enormous psychological resilience. He overcame great adversity with outstanding character and integrity.

However, most resilient people are not famous. Most resilient people are unknown or relatively unknown. How many have heard of Hortense Sneckelgrubber or Beulah Goose-Feathers?

Story 2: Liz Murray

The television movie, *From Homeless to Harvard,* tells the story of Liz Murray who grew up in poverty in New York City's Bronx. Her parents were drug addicts. Most of the families' welfare monies were spent on drugs. Liz and her sister searched garbage dumpsters for food to survive. Liz recalled the time that her mother sold her sister's winter coat which resulted in the sister missing school the next day. Murray pumped gas at self-service stores for tips. At mealtime, she and her sister would follow the smell of food cooking in the apartments of neighbors. They knocked on the doors of neighbors whose food smelled best and asked for a handout. Liz was homeless off and on during her teens. She slept on the streets, on subways, in parks, and at neighbors' homes.

When Liz was sixteen-years-old, her mother died of AIDS. Her mother was given a pauper's funeral. She, her sister, and a friend scrapped together enough money for cab fare for the hour's drive to the cemetery. The mother's name was misspelled and written with a magic marker on top of the pine coffin. Her friend corrected the spelling and wrote "Beloved Mother" then drew an angel.

At that point, Liz said that her view of life changed. She re-evaluated her life and realized that, in a way, she had been depending too much upon others and that she had a window of opportunity to make something of her life and must take action. Only she could change her destiny. She decided to live each day with "purpose."

She battled to gain enrollment into an alternative high school and was given an opportunity to graduate from high school. She studied diligently and graduated at an accelerated pace.

On a field trip to Harvard University, she was impressed with the prestigious school and aspired to attend, realizing that a degree would insure a major head start on the road to success. Upon graduation from high school, *The New York Times* awarded her a scholarship. The scholarship was given to students with good academic credentials who had overcome difficult life obstacles. Liz's dream came true. She earned a scholarship to Harvard. After completing much of her coursework, she took leave to care for her father who was dying of AIDS.

One notable factor is that "Liz's Story," which was her written account of her life, was printed in *The New York Times.* The story created much publicity which brought attention to Liz. First, the community responded, and then the publicity set off a train of events that led to a book and movie.

Liz Murray is now a motivational speaker and hopes that by telling her life story that it can help others overcome obstacles and in some way find meaning in their lives. She notes that she does not wish for others to view her rags-to-riches story as glamorous because it was not. It was filled with hardship and struggle.

Interestingly, she does not cite poverty, hunger, or homelessness as being among her most painful memories. Nor did she blame her parents, though they used food money to buy drugs and would "shoot up" in front of her and her sister. In interviews, the memories that she described as most disturbing were others. For instance, she cites the experience when panhandling and her peers would take out their "mall money" and count it in her presence to taunt her. In addition, she remembers in early life being sent to school dirty and smelly and the other children snickering and avoiding her.

When asked how she survived, she stated that she always loved and felt loved by her mother and father. She fondly remembers her mother tucking her in bed and singing and her father teaching her to appreciate reading. Further, she noted that her parents had taught her how not to live her life.

Comments:

Murray's story is one of turning tragedy into triumph. What was the source of her strength?

In *The Invulnerable Child*, the authors, James and Cohler, observe that invulnerable children seem to develop survival skills and strategies that come from nowhere. They seem to reach deep inside themselves and grasp and mold internal strengths.

From studying paratroop survivors from perilous combat in World War II and Korea, Dr. Al Siebert, resilience researcher, observed that there are lessons in life that cannot be taught but that can be learned. People are often exposed to environments in which they may or may not learn. Sometimes students take what they have been taught by professors and build upon it and go far beyond the teachers' understanding. The exposure to the professor served as a stimulus. Liz learned from her parents both because of and in spite of their example.

Albert Bandura would likely refer to Liz as one with high self-efficacy. Self-efficacy refers to persons' beliefs that they can organize and execute action necessary to successfully achieve a task or goal. It is the belief that people can act in ways to cause an effect upon their environment. Those with high self-efficacy are more likely to exert greater energy and are more persistent in their effort. Self-efficacy is the belief that people have in their abilities and skills. Those with low self-efficacy may feel helpless and that there is no use to try. The belief may be excessively high or low and thus unrealistic. Optimally, self-efficacy should be challenging but realistic— within a range that is achievable.

Attachment theorists such as Bowlby and Ainsworth, would likely view Liz as someone whose basic emotional needs were met. She knew that she had been loved; therefore, she was free to act independently and explore possibilities. In interview after interview, Murray stated that she felt genuine love from her parents and had always loved them. I cannot explain it, but I believe her. No one completely knows what occurs in another's mind, body, or relationships. Knowing, experiencing, authentic love frees one from clinging and feeling hopeless, helpless, and dependent. Feeling genuinely loved brings security.

Years ago, I consulted at a children's home. Some residents were orphans but many had parents who did not care for them. The Department of Human Services had taken the children from their parents. Some of the children had known experiences similar to Liz Murray's. Based upon clinical observation, after interviewing and counseling hundreds of children, it occurred to me that if a child had one person who authentically loved them, that they were likely to face and deal with most life hardships and survive.

By love, I mean someone who has the child's best interest at heart and is willing to sacrifice for the child. People may be told that they are loved while being emotionally or physically abused. For children such mixed messages are especially confusing and the communications promote pathology. To me when people, especially children, are not loved it is much more damaging to be falsely told that they are loved than to truly be told that they are not loved.

Knowing or having known genuine love adds immensely to resiliency. Ideally, children should grow up in homes where they are authentically loved by both parents. However, sometimes it is only one parent, a grandparent, an aunt, an older sibling, a parental substitute or a mentor who loves the child. While knowing love is especially important to children in formative years, it is important for adults as well. The Doobie Brothers asked, "Without love, where would you be now?"

In interviews, Liz often commented about her astonishment at the power of the media. Of course, she was referring to the powerful New York City media. What if she were raised in what some arrogant elitists refer to as "fly-over country" (the Midwest, South, and much of the West)? If she were from Turkey, Texas or even Walla Walla, Washington, I doubt if her story would be known.

However, I imagine that she would be basically the same person. My guess is that she would have completed a GED and received grants and scholarships and worked her way through college. Then she may have married and raised a healthy family and have had a successful career.

Her family and friends would deeply respect her but it would be unlikely, though not impossible, that she would have ever had an opportunity to publish her memoirs or make a movie. If she had sent out prospectuses, odds are that she would have a stack of rejection notices. Would that have made an essential difference in the significance of her life?

Conclusion: Addendum II

Do you know someone whose resiliency led them to overcome great obstacles and to beat the odds? I expect that each of us knows and can name at least one person who is relatively obscure and overcame enormous barriers. Many could name several people who have overcome impediments and obstructions and have not only survived but have thrived.

Addendum III:
Recommendations
Nikki

A leader in the movement to focus upon psychological health and well-being is Martin Seligman. His work led to establishing the Positive Psychology Center at the University of Pennsylvania which in turn has led to establishing other Positive Psychology Centers.

How did Dr. Seligman become interested in psychological wellness and mental health as opposed to mental illness? In an article in *American Psychologist* (2000) he told of a significant transforming event. It was a turning point in his life, and furthermore, changed his perspective of psychology. The experience resulted in his focusing his work more upon positive psychology.

Story: Nikki

Seligman was weeding his garden one day, proceeding at a hurried pace. His daughter, Nikki, was nearby. While he frantically pulled weeds, she danced, sang, and tossed weeds into the air. He scolded her for something and she left, only to return shortly and announce that she wanted to speak to her father.

She asked her dad, "Do you remember when I was three? From the time I was three-years-old until my fifth birthday, I whined a lot. When I turned five I decided to stop whining and did." She went on to explain that changing the habit of whining was the hardest task that she had ever accomplished. Then Nikki concluded, "Daddy, if I could quit whining, you could stop being such a grouch."

Dr. Seligman described the event as a "genuine epiphany." He acknowledged that he had been a grouch and had been difficult to live with. Though a famous, accomplished psychologist, he had not enjoyed life a great deal. He decided at the moment to change just as Nikki had. Not only did the experience modify his behavior, and his view of child rearing, it fundamentally changed his approach to the study of psychology.

Seligman had previously developed the terms, "learned helplessness" and "learned optimism" however the experience with Nikki led to his directing his research toward positive psychology. His research turned from "fixing what is wrong" with people to identifying, nurturing, and encouraging people's strengths.

Comments:

It is my belief that most healthy parents learn as much from their children as they teach their children. Though less than ideal, there must have been a basic rapport between Nikki and her father in order for her to assert herself to him. Nikki was secure enough to approach her father, which is a quality of effective parenting.

Is it not interesting that some changes take decades while others occur in an instant? On occasion, a window of opportunity is open or circumstances catch us off guard to the point that an insight penetrates our defenses. At the time, Seligman was about as high as one can climb on the "psychological status ladder," yet his young daughter made a comment that dramatically changed his life. It not only changed his life, and I would think that of his family, but also it energized a significant movement within the discipline of psychology.

Recommendations

In a presentation at the annual American Psychological Association meeting in 2006, Dr. Martin Seligman identified six research-based exercises that have proven to be effective in positive psychotherapy.

1. Identify five personal strengths. Reflect upon how you can use them more in your daily life.

2. List three blessings, good happenings, that occur each day. Discuss your beliefs about why they occurred.

3. Write an obituary. Project that your life has ended and that it was fulfilling and complete. How would you like to be remembered?

4. Make a gratitude visit. Write a letter to someone to whom you are grateful and have not thanked. Read it to them in person or over the phone.

5. Daily, find an opportunity to react in a demonstratively positive manner to the good fortune of another. It may be good

news that another shares with you or something that you discover about someone else.

6. Take time to savor an experience each day. Consciously focus upon and enjoy an experience that you ordinarily rush through or to which you usually pay little attention. Savor a bite of food, enjoy a walk, or appreciate the beauty of a flower or tree.

Conclusion: Addendums I-III

There are countless additional stories to be told and much more to be said about psychological resilience. Both can be found in other publications as well as discovered in daily life. My hope is to further engage and embrace both in the future.

Addendum: IV
Resources

Following are a few selected web sources:

Website Sources

APA Help Center
The Road to Resilience
Apahelpcenter.org

Dr. Joan Borysenko
www.joanborysenko.com

Joseph Campbell Foundation
www.jcf.org

Center for Positive Psychology
www.ppc.sas.upenn.edu

Center for Story and Symbol—
Jonathan Young, Ph.D.
www.folkstory

Joseph R. Dunn, website
www.drdunn.net

Health Mind Concepts
Psychological Resilience
Dr. Kam Wong
www.healthmindconcepts.com

Addendum: IV

Humor & Health Journal
www.humor.ch/salameh

Institute for Humanistic Studies
Positive Psychology:
A New Force in Humanistic Psychology
www.humaniststudies.org/enews

International Association
of Positive Psychology
www.ippanetwork.org

Mayo Clinic
www.mayoclinic.com/health/resilience

Orthodoxy Today
Resilience and the Canaanite Women
Fr George Morelli, Ph.D.
www.OrthodoxyToday.org

Positive Psychology Daily News
www.pos-psych.com

Psychology Etcetera
www.PsychEtc.com

Psychological Resilience and Positive
Emotional Granularity
www.faculty.vassar.edu/mitugade

Self-actualization
www.abraham-maslow.com

Al Siebert, Ph.D.
The Resiliency Center
www.resiliencycenter.com

Spirituality
The link between spirituality
and resilience in children
www.findarticles.com

WebMD
Health & Balance
Can you teach resilience?
www.WebMD.com

What is Psychological Resilience?
www.wilderdom.com/psychology/resilience

Note: Additional references and resources on psychological resiliency shall be posted on the web at PsychEtc.com.

About the Author:
More Than You Want to Know

By Guru Jaybird McWalloby

Joseph R. Dunn grew up on a farm in Christian County, Kentucky near the city of Hopkinsville. In addition to being a farmer, his father was an insulation contractor and the son had to work for his dad in the summers. One hot August afternoon, while working in an attic and drenching wet with perspiration and breathing fiberglass insulation, Dunn contends that Jesus called him to become a psychologist. Though no one witnessed the event, the call was realized.

The author currently resides in Jackson, Mississippi and lives a rather quiet, humble existence. He does not even have any pets about which to brag and does not want any.

He holds graduate degrees from Mississippi State University, University of Memphis (formerly Memphis State University, where he had to pay a parking ticket before they would grant him his degree), Harding Graduate School of Religion and an undergraduate degree from Lipscomb University. His study has primarily focused upon psychology with secondary emphasis in theology.

Dr. Dunn taught psychology at Wesley College in Dover, Delaware and at Christian Brothers University in Memphis, Tennessee. He has taught graduate classes as an adjunct (something) for Mississippi State University.

He has served as clinical director at two mental health centers; however most of his professional life has been devoted to private practice in psychology. He has also served as editor and publisher for four periodicals.

Dr. Dunn was founder of the American Association of Christian Counselors (AACC) in 1986. He was publisher and editor of its journals through 1992. He has relinquished his appointment as lifetime member to the Advisory Board and is no longer associated or affiliated with the organization in any manner.

The man loves the study of psychology especially as it relates to multidisciplinary studies, that is, how psychology connects with literature, spirituality, business, and just about everything else.

Dunn is into college football and basketball in addition to humor, mind/body health, biographies, and documentaries. He enjoys the study of history and, of course, teaching stories. He listens to bluegrass, blues, post country, and some classical music.

With great concern, warmth, and candor, his grandmother used to say, "Joe Richard, you are a 'curious' boy." By "curious" she meant strange or peculiar. She was definitely correct; however, he is curious in the traditional sense as well.

Dunn loves his mother and family and they not only tolerate him but seem to hold genuine affection. He has grandchildren about whom to brag and bore others. In addition, he is blessed with a few close friends. He philosophizes, "That's about all I can hope for in this life except for a good woman and a winning football team to support." Regarding the former, he confides that he could not trust the judgment of anyone who would live with him.

Journals by the Author

Publisher and Editor: *The Christian Journal of Psychology and Counseling* (1986-1992)

Publisher and Editor: *Counseling Today* (Audio Journal) 1986-1992

Publisher and Editor: *Humor & Health Journal* (1992-2000)

Editor: *Psychology and Health Online Journal* (2000-2005)

Other Publications

Humor & Health: An Overview of Research, Literature, and Clinical Discoveries with Practical Applications and Recommendations
(Three Volume Audio Cassette Tapes)

I Hope My Son Turns Out as Well as I Meant to
(Cartoons and Clip-toons)

Great Quotes that I Wish I'd Thought of but Didn't: Humorous Quotes Collected by JRD

There's No Law Against Laughing
(Audio Tape)

Emotional Wisdom: Lessons From Teaching Stories
by Waleed A. Salameh, Ph.D.
Interviewed, produced, and edited
by Joseph R. Dunn

Contact/Order Information

I thoroughly enjoy communicating with readers, students, authors, psychotherapists, interviewers, and others interested in stories and their applications—including wealthy entrepreneurs, travelling troubadours, and handsome Gypsy women. However, please bear in mind the reality of time constraints and do not be insulted if I am unable to respond in the manner that I would prefer. I shall be available as time permits.

Mail: POB 16996, Jackson, MS 39236
Email: PsychEtc@gmail.com
Phone: (601) 957-0075
www.PsychEtc.com or drdunn.net

Check website for eBook edition

P.S. Unfortunately, Dr. Dunn's Chief of Staff and Literary Agent, Guru Jaybird Beauregard McWalloby, is currently on sabbatical conducting highly classified research under the auspices of the Department of Corrections. He is only available for visiting hours on weekends.

However, please be advised that anyone who abuses this information for sales, junk mail, telemarketing, requests, for "love offerings" or other inappropriate reasons is subject to "enjoying" a visit from Jaybird's brothers. The McWalloby boys are "set well" and some folk describe them as "ornery and no-account." The boys are not very resilient and do not like to talk. They prefer nonverbal means of communication. The brothers live in a trailer hooked to a truck with a Cummins Diesel and are highly mobile.

CPSIA information can be obtained at www.ICGtesting.com
228294LV00006B/81/P

9 780578 011561